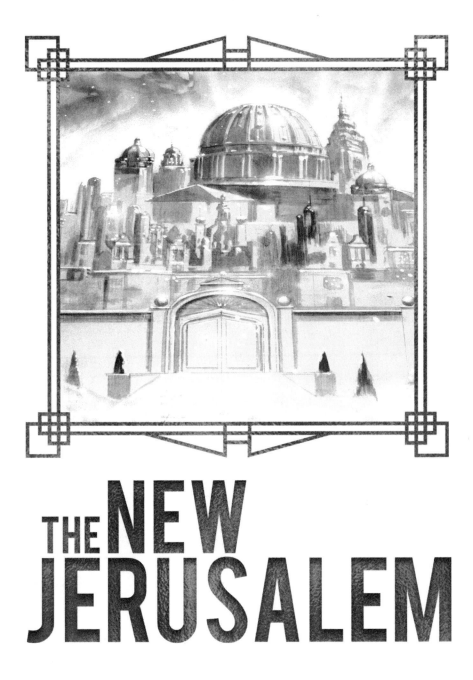

THE NEW JERUSALEM

THE NEW JERUSALEM

JIMMY SWAGGART

JIMMY SWAGGART MINISTRIES

P.O. Box 262550 | Baton Rouge, Louisiana 70826-2550

www.jsm.org

ISBN 978-1-941403-32-7
09-143 | COPYRIGHT © 2016 Jimmy Swaggart Ministries®
16 17 18 19 20 21 22 23 24 25 / EBM / 10 9 8 7 6 5 4 3 2 1

TABLE OF CONTENTS

THE NEW JERUSALEM

INTRODUCTION

INTRODUCTION

THE FUTURE OF THIS planet called Earth is very much in the thinking of many people. Global warming is a tremendous part of all of that.

Some claim that the climate is gradually getting warmer until it will ultimately bake this planet, thereby, little by little destroying it completely. Others claim that instead of a gradual warming, actually, the planet is entering into a time when the temperature is dropping. Those who favor the increase in temperature claim that man is the culprit, with his automobiles, etc.

THE BIBLE

In reality, the Word of God—the Bible—is the only book in the world that gives us the future of this planet called Earth. Admittedly, some dark days are just ahead. It's called the great tribulation. Jesus said that it would be worse than anything this world has ever seen before (Mat. 24:21). However, this terrible time will last for a period of seven years, with the far worst being the last three and a half years.

During that time, there is a possibility that nearly half the population will die; however, it will not be caused by global warming, etc. Rather, it will be caused by war and, as well, the Lord using the elements to bring judgment. In fact, the Scripture says of that particular time, *"For the great day of His wrath is come* (the wrath of God); *and who shall be able to stand?"* (Rev. 6:17).

As well, the Lord has promised that before this terrible time comes upon this earth, He will take out of this world all who are born again. It's called the rapture of the church (I Thess. 4:13-18). This terrible time will conclude with the second coming of the Lord, which will introduce the thousand-year kingdom age. Jesus will be ruling in person the entirety of this planet as King of kings and Lord of lords for the entirety of its 1,000 years. At that time the world will know peace and prosperity as it has never known before, and that means the entirety of the world and not just a part of it.

THE PERFECT AGE TO COME

As wonderful as that thousand-year reign is going to be, it will be nothing by comparison to what is going to take place after that. Actually, the last happening will last forever and forever. God will transfer His headquarters from planet Heaven to planet Earth, where it will remain forever. The mighty oceans at that time will be no more, with the world left with rivers, streams, lakes, etc.

Where some five-sixths of the planet is now covered by water, that will be reduced to probably one-sixth, counting the lakes, rivers, etc.

THE NEW JERUSALEM

To give you an example of the greatness and the glory of the New Jerusalem that will come down from God out of heaven, the Scripture tells us that it is approximately 1,500 miles wide and 1,500 miles long. In other words, if you put the southeastern footprint in Dallas, Texas, the southwestern footprint in Los Angeles, California, the northwestern footprint in Vancouver, British Columbia, Canada, and the northeastern footprint in Minneapolis, Minnesota, that would be approximately the size of this city. That's not all; the best is yet to come.

Not only will it be 1,500 miles wide and 1,500 miles long, it will also be 1,500 miles high (Rev. 21:16). This is what God has prepared for them who love Him (I Cor. 2:9-10).

I pray that the Lord will help us in the writing of this book to at least somewhat adequately portray the glory and the grandeur of it all, and yes, it will be eternal. That is the future of planet Earth.

On Jordan's stormy banks I stand
And cast a wishful eye
To Canaan's fair and happy land,
Where my possessions lie.

Over all those wide extended plains
Shines one eternal day;
There God the Son forever reigns
And scatters night away.

No chilling winds nor poisonous breath
Can reach that healthful shore;
Sickness and sorrow, pain and death
Are felt and feared no more.

When shall I reach that happy place,
And be forever blest?
When shall I see my Father's face,
And in His bosom rest?

THE NEW JERUSALEM

CHAPTER 1

THE NEW HEAVEN AND THE NEW EARTH

THE NEW HEAVEN
AND THE NEW EARTH

"AND I SAW A new heaven and a new earth: for the first heaven and the first earth were passed away; and there was no more sea" (Rev. 21:1).

A NEW HEAVEN AND A NEW EARTH

Other than John, the phrase, *"And I saw a new heaven and a new earth,"* is mentioned only by Isaiah and Simon Peter.

The Lord through the ancient prophet said, *"For, behold, I create new heavens and a new earth: and the former shall not be remembered, nor come into mind"* (Isa. 65:17).

He then said, *"For as the new heavens and the new earth, which I will make, shall remain before Me, says the LORD, so shall your seed and your name remain"* (Isa. 66:22).

Peter said, *"Nevertheless we, according to His promise, look for new heavens and a new earth, wherein dwells righteousness"* (II Pet. 3:13).

HOW THE NEW HEAVENS AND THE NEW
EARTH WILL BE BROUGHT ABOUT

Peter also said:

But the day of the Lord will come as a thief in the night; in the which the heavens shall pass away with a great noise, and the elements shall melt with fervent heat, the earth also and the works that are therein shall be burned up. Seeing then that all these things shall be dissolved, what manner of persons ought ye to be in all holy con- versation and godliness, looking for and hasting unto the coming of the day of God, wherein the heavens being on fire shall be dissolved, and the elements shall melt with fervent heat? (II Pet. 3:10-12).

This will take place at the conclusion of the thousand-year kingdom age (II Pet. 3:7).

"Pass away" in verse 10 in the Greek is *parerchomai* and means "to pass from one condition to another." It never means annihilation. It does not indicate the elimination of heaven and earth, but rather a remaking of heaven and earth.

New in the Greek is *kainos* and means "freshness with respect to age." The idea is this: When finished, it will be new, as is obvious, but the beautiful thing is, it will remain new and fresh forever and forever. This is because there will be no sin to cause corruption, which incorporates itself now in everything. Only God could build something in that manner.

PASSED AWAY

The phrase, *"For the first heaven and the first earth were passed away,"* refers to the original creation. It has been marred by sin and shame; therefore, it is necessary to completely eliminate the old surface and bring into existence a brand-new surface.

The word *heaven* as used here doesn't refer to the abode of God, but rather the atmospheric heavens around the earth. The idea pertains to the pollution these heavens have experienced, and above all, the fact that demon spirits have occupied this region basically for the entirety of human history (Eph. 2:2). That is due to the fall. So, all of this will be cleansed by fire, thereby, making a new heaven and a new earth.

Peter said,*"But the heavens and the earth, which are now, by the same word are kept in store, reserved unto fire against the day of judgment and perdition of ungodly men"* (II Pet. 3:7).

NO MORE SEA

The phrase, *"And there was no more sea,"* refers to the giant oceans, such as the Pacific and the Atlantic. There will continue to be lakes, bodies of water, rivers, streams, etc. The great seas and oceans presently occupy nearly three-fourths of the globe's surface, and to that extent, they prevent occupation by men, except for the comparatively small number who are mariners.

The idea is that the whole world will then be habitable, and no part will be given up to vast oceans, although there will still be bodies of water, as stated. They will be strategically placed, providing not only beauty but, as well, contributing to the overall benefit of the entirety of the planet.

The present oceans make their contribution, as well; however, their vastness severely limits the possibilities of life and living as it regards the population of the world. The new earth will, no doubt, have the blessing of many, many bodies of water with its rivers, lakes, and waterfalls, but it will not suffer the loss of vast areas of land.

THE MILLIONS ON EARTH

At the time of this great change, there will be untold millions of people on this earth. This will include all the glorified saints, which will, no doubt, number into many millions. It will also include Israel, along with all the Gentiles who accepted Christ during the kingdom age. None of these (Jews or Gentiles) will have glorified bodies but will still be inhabitants of this earth.

What will the Lord do with this vast number while the heaven and the earth are being renovated by fire?

There's only one answer of which I am aware. The Lord will take everyone to heaven, there to await this wonderful renovation. As we come to the conclusion of the Word of God, and looking at our own experiences that affect each of us, I'm sure that we understand by now that the Lord can do anything.

As Christ said, *"With God all things are possible"* (Mat. 19:26).

NEW JERUSALEM

"And I John saw the Holy City, New Jerusalem, coming down from God out of heaven, prepared as a bride adorned for her husband" (Rev. 21:2).

The phrase, *"And I John saw the Holy City, New Jerusalem,"* presents for this new earth a new city. In Matthew 4:5 and 27:53, Jerusalem is referred to as *"the Holy City."* It is not referred to again as such until Revelation 11:2. No doubt, this is because of the rejection of her Messiah, the Lord Jesus Christ.

Each and every city in the world presently is filled with sin, shame, murder, heartache, and suffering. It is filled with death and dying, and with that is coupled loneliness, even extreme loneliness. The city that John describes here is new, meaning that it is not touched by sin, shame, or anything that sin may bring about. Such no longer exists.

Even the kingdom age will not be able to compare with the perfect age. In fact, it will not be possible for the New Jerusalem to be brought down until the heaven and the earth are cleansed by fire. Every vestige of pollution, sin, and shame has to be cleansed before such can be done.

THE FALL

Going back to the fall, man was dispossessed of all that God intended for him. It was the purpose of God that man would have total dominion, not only of this earth, but of all of God's creation, but sin cursed this purpose and, thereby, destroyed this dream.

Due to the fall and the terrible entrance of sin into this world, man is doomed to earn his living by the sweat of his brow, and to do so in a world of death and misery. He watches as youthfulness turns to age, and with even all of vaunted modern science, there is nothing he can do about it. He must ultimately go back to the dust of the ground out of which he was made. This is the curse of sin in the earth.

Let the reader understand that as far as sin has destroyed, just as far does redemption go, and then beyond! Because of sin, man has been dispossessed from his rightful dominion, but in grace, God will restore to man the lost creation. Whatever sin has polluted, dirtied, and soiled, redemption will cleanse. Whatever sin has wasted, God's grace will abound in glorious regeneration and renovation. There will be a new heaven, a new earth, and a new city.

THE CROSS

Let the reader also understand that when we read here about the new heaven and the new earth, and, as well, about this glorious New Jerusalem, we must forever know that all of this has been made possible by what Jesus did at the Cross. The Holy Spirit reminds us of this in verse 9. The Cross is the means of redemption and, thereby, makes it possible for the life of redemption to cover every vestige of the death of sin. In fact, in these last two chapters of Revelation, which describe the perfect age, the name *Lamb* is used seven times. To be sure, this is done by the Holy Spirit for a purpose. He wants us to understand that all of this that is coming—the beauty, the glory, the power, the wonder, and the perfection—all, and without exception, has been made possible by what Jesus did at the Cross. It must never be forgotten!

OUT OF HEAVEN

The phrase, *"coming down from God out of heaven,"* proclaims the fact that this world will never evolve a golden age or ideal state. The New Jerusalem must descend from God. The true pattern, which alone will realize man's highest wishes, can only come from God, our Creator and Redeemer. Man cannot produce such, irrespective of how hard he tries.

Salvation and redemption came from heaven. Grace and glory have come from heaven. The baptism with the Holy Spirit has come from heaven. Eternal life has come from heaven. And now, the New Jerusalem, the dwelling place of the redeemed, comes from heaven as well! It is God who must do the doing, or it is not done.

A BRIDE

The phrase, *"prepared as a bride adorned for her husband,"* proclaims as a dwelling place the eternal home of the redeemed. The word *prepared* probably harks back to Jesus' promise to prepare a place in His Father's house for His own (Jn. 14:2-3).

Some have tried to limit the New Jerusalem as the home of the church alone; however, it evidently includes all the redeemed of all ages.

Paul wrote, *"We know that if our earthly house of this tabernacle were dissolved, we have a building of God, an house not made with hands, eternal in the heavens"* (II Cor. 5:1). The terminology given here by the apostle, and more particularly, given by the Holy Spirit, includes all redeemed and not just a select group.

The phrase, *"prepared as a bride adorned for her husband,"* refers to the fact that this city is prepared especially for the redeemed. While the angelic host will definitely have access and will, no doubt, function greatly in this city, still, it is prepared especially for the redeemed.

A GREAT VOICE

"And I heard a great voice out of heaven saying, Behold, the tabernacle of God is with men, and He will dwell with them, and they shall be His people, and God Himself shall be with them, and be their God" (Rev. 21:3).

The phrase, *"And I heard a great voice out of heaven,"* proclaims the last time this term is used of the 21 times it is used in this book of Revelation. The word *a* denotes both importance and urgency.

According to the best manuscripts, the voice now heard was heard out of the throne, giving it even more power and strength.

This great voice will proclaim a message of unprecedented proportions. It will be that which will satisfy the longing heart of man, and do so forever and forever. What this great voice says is what will make the New Jerusalem wonderful and glorious.

THE TABERNACLE OF GOD

The phrase, *"Behold, the tabernacle of God is with men, and He will dwell with them, and they shall be His people, and God Himself shall be with them, and be their God,"* finally proclaims that which God intended all along.

It is amazing concerning the parallels in the opening chapters of the Bible with those near the close. The Lord God is said to be walking in the garden and to be present among the trees of the garden (Gen. 3:8). It is the horror of sin that has disrupted the union between God and man. In fact, spiritual death, which was caused by sin, is the separation of man from God. However, immediately, God set about to restore this union, even though it would take some 7,000 years to do such, at least as described here.

Down through the centuries of the Word of God, we see the Lord ever coming closer.

GOD DWELLS WITH MAN

In order that a thrice-holy God might have fellowship with sinful man, the sacrificial system was instituted at the very

beginning, which, as a portrayal of the great redemption process, pictured Jesus dying on the Cross (Gen. 4:4). The sacrificial process of communion with God remained for some
2,500 years.

The Lord then gave to Moses the plan for the tabernacle,
which included the Holy of Holies, where the ark of the
covenant and the mercy seat were, with the cherubims at each
end. Concerning that, the Lord said, *"And there I will meet
with you, and I will commune with you from above the mercy
seat, from between the two cherubims which are upon the
ark of the testimony, of all things which I will give you in
commandment unto the children of Israel"* (Ex. 25:22).

Then, some 500 years later, the Lord chose a city—
Jerusalem—where He would place His name and, as well,
have a temple built there in which He would dwell (II
Chron. 6:6, 10).

After the Cross, which was about 1,000 years after the
building of the temple, the Holy Spirit then came to dwell permanently in the hearts and lives of believers (Jn. 14:16-17).
As should be obvious, the Lord is ever drawing closer to that
which He desires to do: *"He will dwell with them."*

GOD HIMSELF

At the second coming, Christ will, as well, come down to
dwell with men (Zech. 14:4). Even though Christ will then
reign personally, the situation still will not be ideal simply because of the fact that sin remains, although in a limited manner.

But then, the heaven and the earth will be renovated by fire, thereby, cleansed from the practical results of sin, even as the Cross cleansed from the spiritual results of sin. Then the New Jerusalem will come down from God out of heaven, which, in effect, means that God has transferred His throne from heaven to earth. He will then dwell with men permanently and be their God, which means there will be no other gods.

The expression, *"God Himself,"* is significant because this implies that here is the final consummation of all things.

Concerning this, Paul said: *"Then comes the end, when He* (Christ) *shall have delivered up the kingdom to God, even the Father; when He shall have put down all rule and all authority and power ... And when all things shall be subdued unto Him, then shall the Son also Himself be subject unto Him who put all things under Him, that God may be all in all"* (I Cor. 15:24, 28).

Once again we emphasize that all of this is made possible by what Jesus did at the Cross. That should be overly obvious to every believer, and if not, then the Word of God is not being interpreted properly. The story of the Bible is the story of man's redemption, and redemption was brought about by the Cross of Christ. We might quickly add that all redemption was and is brought about by the Cross of Christ.

NO MORE TEARS

"And God shall wipe away all tears from their eyes; and there shall be no more death, neither sorrow, nor crying,

neither shall there be any more pain: for the former things are passed away" (Rev. 21:4).

The phrase, *"And God shall wipe away all tears from their eyes,"* actually says in the Greek, "every teardrop." This refers to tears of heartache, sorrow, pain, and suffering, which have bathed the faces of every human being who has ever lived, and has done so in copious ways.

This will be one of the characteristics of that blessed state—that not a tear of sorrow or heartache shall ever be shed there.

All tears have come from sin's distortion of God's purposes for man. An enemy has done this to the original order. Then, God will have defeated the enemy and liberated His people and His creation.

The story of this world is a story of bereavement. Jesus wept with Mary and Martha at the tomb of their brother. Here on this earth is misfortune and poverty, even as Lazarus, the righteous one, but yet, a beggar, was laid at the door of the rich man, who, incidentally, was unrighteous. This means that the inequities abound, and to be sure, these inequities bring the tears.

However, one day, that's all going to be over. God Himself will wipe the tears from our faces, even every teardrop, and that will be the end of that!

Let the reader understand that the wiping away of every teardrop is not actually referring to a literal cleansing of the face. It is referring to all the sorrow and heartache caused by tears. Only Christ could address the cause, which He did at Calvary. At salvation, we experience the firstfruits of the atonement; at the resurrection, the totality; however, all sorrow and heartache cannot truly be said to be gone forever until the time of the new heaven and the new earth when the New Jerusalem will come down from God out of heaven. All sin will then not only be gone, but all effects of sin as well!

THE AGONIZING QUARTET

The phrase, *"And there shall be no more death, neither sorrow, nor crying, neither shall there be any more pain,"* addresses sin and all its results. This mentioned is what causes the tears, and with all of it taken away, there will be no more tears or cause for tears.

Chapter 3 of Genesis tells us of the coming into the world of death, sorrow, crying, and pain. Here, in the next to the last chapter of the Bible, we have the promise that they shall be no more.

When we think of this, our minds span the nearly 6,000 years of recorded history between the entrance of sin into this world and its finish. And yet, we must realize that we are living presently on the very eve of the great change that is about to come.

Death is an enemy, and it will be the last enemy defeated (I Cor. 15:26). It was caused by sin, i.e., separation from God. God made Adam and Eve to live forever, and this they would have done had not sin entered the picture. Even then, the physical bodies of that time, which were so wonderfully created, took nearly 1,000 years to die. To be sure, the ages given in Genesis, Chapter 5, are not fictitious. These people actually lived that long. Such will again come back during the kingdom age, and, of course, all believers will live forever.

Jesus said: *"I am the resurrection, and the life: he who believes in Me, though he were dead, yet shall he live: And whosoever lives and believes in Me shall never die"* (Jn. 11:25-26).

Victory over death was made possible by the Cross. Jesus died that we might live!

SORROW

Concerning sorrow, the Lord said to Eve upon the advent of her terrible fall, *"In sorrow you shall bring forth children"* (Gen. 3:16).

The idea is that sorrow would plague the child from its infancy to the time it died, and so it has been, and so it is.

Crying comes from the sorrow.

The pain addressed here refers not only to physical pain but, as well, to the pain of a broken heart.

Jesus addressed all of this at the beginning of His ministry. He said:

The Spirit of the Lord is upon Me, because He has anointed Me to preach the gospel (good news) *to the poor* (poor respecting money and poor of spirit); *He has sent Me to heal the brokenhearted* (the sorrows of life), *to preach deliverance to the captives* (we are delivered by trusting in what Christ did at the Cross), *and recovering of sight to the blind* (spiritual sight), *to set at liberty them who are bruised* (the bruises of life imprison the spirit of man), *to preach the acceptable year of the Lord* (the Year of Jubilee) (Lk. 4:18-19) (The Expositor's Study Bible).

If it is to be noticed, all of these things are spiritual. As well, all were made possible at the Cross!

FORMER THINGS

In Revelation 21:4, the phrase, *"for the former things are passed away,"* refers to the entirety of the effects of the fall. Things will now be as God formerly intended for them to be. None of these types of former things were His will! Now, in totality and completeness, and into perpetuity, the prayer of Christ will be answered: *"Your kingdom come. Your will be done in earth, as it is in heaven"* (Mat. 6:10).

THE THRONE

"And He who sat upon the throne said, Behold, I make all things new. And He said unto me, Write: for these words are true and faithful" (Rev. 21:5).

The phrase, *"And He who sat upon the throne said,"* presents God Himself as the speaker for the second time in this book. From His throne comes the assurance that the One who created the first heaven and earth will indeed make all things new. Since these words are in truth God's words, it is of utmost importance that this vision of the new heaven and the New Jerusalem be proclaimed to the churches. He actually says seven things in this message to John and, in reality, to all believers.

NEW

The phrase, *"Behold, I make all things new,"* proclaims His first word.

Two words for *new* are used in the New Testament, but there is a difference between them. The one contemplates the object spoken of under the aspect of something that has newly been brought into existence. The other word speaks of that which has previously existed but has been outworn and is now given a fresh aspect. The latter word is employed here.

TRUE AND FAITHFUL

The phrase, *"And He said unto me, Write: for these words are true and faithful,"* refers to the second statement made.

This message in its totality must not be forgotten, so John is instructed by the Lord to write it down. He is to understand that what is being said is true and faithful, meaning that it is exactly as the Lord describes, i.e., true. As well, the word *faithful* guarantees that it will all be brought to pass.

The glorious words *true and faithful* are also the name of our Lord but in reverse order.

ALPHA AND OMEGA

"And He said unto me, It is done. I am Alpha and Omega, the beginning and the end. I will give unto him who is athirst of the fountain of the water of life freely" (Rev. 21:6).

The phrase, *"And He said unto me, It is done. I am alpha and omega, the beginning and the end,"* presents the third part of the message.

The same word, *"It is done"* (Rev. 16:17), pronounced the judgment of the world as finished. Now God proclaims with these same words, *"It is done,"* that He has completed His new creation. Let it ever be said that this time, there will be no entrance of Satan and sin as it was after the former re-creation (Gen., Chpt. 3).

The words, *"He said"* (Rev. 21:5-6), assure reality and fulfillment. The heavens and the earth will be revived, but death and the grave never will be. They will never have any power again, for death—the last enemy—is destroyed.

As well, there will no longer be a mediatorial kingdom. God is all in all. Man will be in God's dwelling place. It will be a paradise that nothing can pollute.

The mighty declaration *"finished* ('It is done')" heard at the morning of creation, at Calvary, and now repeated here for the last time closes all prophecy. He, who as the Alpha created the primal heavens, will as the Omega establish the new heavens. What He began, He now will finish.

THE WATER OF LIFE

The phrase, *"I will give unto him who is athirst of the*

fountain of the water of life freely," presents the fourth statement.

This particular statement doesn't refer to the coming perfect age, for all then will have this water of life and, in effect, will always have this commodity. This promise, and it is a promise, was meant to apply to all who would live from John's day forward. Of course, for those who had died previously without the water of life, which all could have had by faith, there was no way that it could now be had. Death always ends the opportunity of salvation.

In fact, this promise stands good even at this very hour, and will stand good even throughout the kingdom age, which is yet to come.

This fountain of the water of life is tied directly to the Cross of Calvary. The prophet Zechariah said concerning this very thing: *"In that day there shall be a fountain opened to the house of David and to the inhabitants of Jerusalem for sin and for uncleanness"* (Zech. 13:1).

There is only one fountain that cleanses from all sin, and that is the precious blood of Christ (I Jn. 1:7).

Once again, the Cross is held up as that which makes possible all things.

THE CROSS

The reader may wonder why I refer to the Cross again and again. I do so because the Holy Spirit, in one way or the other, refers to the Cross again and again throughout the entirety of the Bible. As well, Satan has been very successful in the last several decades at pulling the church away from the Cross. In fact, it is presently so bad that preachers openly repudiate the Cross and refer to it as "past miseries" and "the worst defeat in human history," which the propagators of the Word of Faith doctrine do. And yet, few raise a voice against this gross error. Actually, it is *"doctrines of devils (demons)"* produced by *"seducing spirits"* (I Tim. 4:1).

It doesn't matter how much the name of Jesus is used or how much the Word of God is quoted. If it's not understood that the name of Jesus has its authority in the Cross and, in fact, that the Word of God is the story of the Cross, then such exercise is a fruitless effort. That's what Paul was speaking about when he referred to *"another Jesus,"* which doctrine is brought about by *"another spirit,"* and which produces *"another gospel"* (II Cor. 11:4).

That's why Paul said: *"We preach Christ crucified"* (I Cor. 1:23). It's not enough to merely preach Christ; it must be Christ crucified.

NO ANSWER OUTSIDE OF THE CROSS

This means that there is no answer outside of the Cross, no cleansing outside of the Cross, no healing outside of the Cross, and no deliverance outside of the Cross, in other words, no salvation outside of the Cross. What we are teaching and preaching to you is not something new. In fact, we are doing our very best to teach and preach exactly that which the Lord gave to the apostle Paul, and which the apostle gave to us. I seek not to deviate one iota!

For every Christian who reads these words, let it be known and understood that if you are to walk in victory, then you can do so only through what Christ did at the Cross and faith in that finished work. When I say victory, I mean victory over the world, the flesh, and the Devil, and I mean victory in totality. Making the Cross as the forever object of your faith gives the Holy Spirit latitude in your life (Rom. 8:1-2, 11). In fact, that and that alone gives Him latitude.

This means that millions who have been baptized with the Holy Spirit still do not enjoy His power because they have made something else other than the Cross of Christ the object of their faith.

WHAT THE LORD REVEALED TO ME

The year was 1988 in the month of March, and my world had come to pieces. The only thing I knew to do was pray. I knew that no one had the solution but the Lord, so I continually importuned Him, despite the fact that the majority of the church world was laughing at me and, in effect, telling me that there was no hope from the Lord. I knew there was hope *only* from the Lord.

One particular morning while trying to pray, it seemed that the powers of darkness were excessively heavy at that particular time. In those days, I would almost always pray while walking. We live on some 25 acres outside of the city limits of

Baton Rouge, Louisiana. Both my home and Donnie's home are located on these 25 acres.

Satan fought so hard that morning that words would actually fail me if I would attempt to describe his actions. Suffice to say, it was unbearable. He taunted me as only he can do, telling me that it was hopeless and that I was wasting my time. But thank God, I continued to attempt to implore the Lord.

THE SPIRIT OF GOD

At a point in time, I suppose about 30 minutes after I had begun praying, it happened all of a sudden. The Spirit of God came upon me, which immediately dispelled the powers of darkness. The Lord then began to say some things to me.

Among other things, He told me that morning that He was going to teach me some things about the Holy Spirit that I did not then know.

Of course, there were many things I didn't know about the Holy Spirit; He is God! However, the Lord was answering the cry of my heart as it regarded the working and moving of the Holy Spirit within my life pertaining to the problem at hand. I had seen literally hundreds of thousands, and I exaggerate not, brought to a saving knowledge of Jesus Christ, which, of course, is a direct result of the moving and operation of the Holy Spirit. As well, I had seen tens of thousands baptized with the Holy Spirit, and again I exaggerate not! So, if the Holy Spirit helped me in one of the greatest efforts of evangelism the world had ever known, and I speak the truth, why

wouldn't He help me as it regarded attacks against me personally by Satan? I didn't understand that, and now the Lord told
me that He was going to explain this to me as it regarded the
Holy Spirit.

NINE YEARS

And yet, it would be approximately nine years before
this answer would come. In fact, for the answer to come,
the Lord had to shut me up strictly unto Himself and away
from the rudiments of the world, or anything else for that
matter. He told me to begin two prayer meetings a day. This
was in 1991. He told me that during these times of prayer, I
was to seek Him more so for who He was than for what He
could do. In other words, a greater relationship had to be
established.

During those six years, and especially those six years of
concentrated prayer, the Lord gave me promise after promise, but yet, never related to me the answer for which I sought.
Then in 1997, it came, and the moment it came, I knew it was
the answer, and I knew it beyond the shadow of a doubt.

The Lord first took me to Romans, Chapter 6, and literally explained it to me. He then said to me, "The answer
for which you seek is found only in the Cross." Then a few
days later, He beautifully gave me the answer concerning the
Holy Spirit for which I had so long sought, but let the reader
understand that the understanding of the Cross had to precede that.

THE WAY THE HOLY SPIRIT WORKS

For the answer regarding the Spirit and how that He helps us in our own personal lives, the Lord took me to Romans 8:2. The reader must remember that Chapter 8 of Romans cannot really be understood unless one first of all understands Romans, Chapter 6. He showed me the following three things:

1. He told me that all things come to the believer through Christ and the Cross (I Cor. 1:17-18, 21, 23; 2:2, 5).

2. He told me that the object of my faith must always be the Cross. This is very, very important (Rom. 6:3-14; Col. 2:10-15; Gal. 6:14).

3. He showed me that by understanding the Cross and always making it the object of faith, the Holy Spirit can then mightily work within our lives and give us victory over all things (Rom. 8:1-2, 11).

From that time, my whole world has changed; my life has changed; and my message has changed, or I should say, become more complete. As well, my understanding of the Word of God has changed, and again I should say, become more complete.

Thank God that the Lord has done exactly what He said that He would do. Now I'm doing everything I know to do to preach this Message of the Cross to all who will hear and believe (Rev. 3:13). Of course, I'm doing it with His help and guidance.

FREELY

I think I can say that the one word *freely* sums up all of

this that I've said more than any other word. How is that so?

Almost every Christian in the world would heartily agree that the things of the Lord are given to us freely; however, by not understanding the Cross, they turn right around and attempt to earn what all the time they are claiming is free. I know; I've been there!

As the sinner cannot earn salvation, neither can the Christian earn sanctification, and that's where the rub comes in. Again, almost every Christian will agree that the sinner cannot earn salvation, but it's another story when it comes to their thinking as it regards sanctification.

Sanctification means to be set apart completely from the world and unto God. In its brief sense, it means to have victory over all sin in that sin does not dominate one in any way (Rom. 6:14). While the Bible does not teach sinless perfection, it most definitely does teach that sin is not to have dominion over us.

If the Christian doesn't understand the Cross as it regards our sanctification, in other words, how we live for God on a daily basis, and how we have victory over the world, the flesh, and the Devil, then such a believer is going to live a life of defeat no matter how much that believer loves the Lord.

SANCTIFICATION

At the moment the believing sinner comes to Christ, such a person first of all is sanctified, then justified, and one day will be glorified, and that day will be when the trump sounds.

Paul said:

And such were some of you (before conversion): *but you are washed* (refers to the blood of Jesus cleansing from all sin), *but you are sanctified* (one's position in Christ), *but you are justified* (declared not guilty) *in the name of the Lord Jesus* (refers to Christ and what He did at the Cross in order that we might be saved), *and by the Spirit of our God* (proclaims the third person of the triune Godhead as the mechanic, so to speak, in this great work of grace) (I Cor. 6:11) (The Expositor's Study Bible).

We must understand that we have to be made clean (positional sanctification) before we can be declared clean (justification). When the person comes to Christ, he is instantly made clean and then declared clean. That is positional sanctification.

However, our condition is not nearly up to our position. The position we have in Christ does not change and will not change. Progressive sanctification, in other words, our condition, changes from day to day. It is the business of the Holy Spirit to bring our condition up to our position. To be sure, it is a lifelong process (Mat. 3:11-12).

Paul also said:

And the very God of peace sanctify you wholly (this is 'progressive sanctification,' which can only be brought about by the Holy Spirit, who does such as our faith is firmly anchored in the Cross, within which parameters the Spirit always works; the sanctification process involves the whole man); *and I pray God your whole spirit and soul and body* (proclaims the make-up of the whole man) *be preserved blameless unto the coming of our Lord Jesus Christ* (I Thess. 5:23) (The Expositor's Study Bible).

So, as believers, we have positional sanctification, which is what is given to us upon our conversion to Christ, and progressive sanctification, which is a work of the Holy Spirit, and which, as stated, is a lifelong project.

Of course, the Holy Spirit is also very much involved in positional sanctification, as should be obvious. So, as a believer, you are sanctified, and at the same time, you are being sanctified.

As should be obvious, sanctification is extremely important, but yet, that of which most Christians have little understanding.

THE BELIEVER'S PART IN PROGRESSIVE SANCTIFICATION

This is so important that the Holy Spirit through the apostle Paul designated that about 98 percent of all of his writings in his 14 epistles be dedicated to the subject of progressive sanctification. That's how important it is. So, how is the believer to function in this capacity?

Let us say at the first that the way, and the only way, that we can grow in grace and the knowledge of the Lord is to place our faith exclusively (I said exclusively) in Christ and what Christ has done for us at the Cross. Growing in grace and the knowledge of the Lord refers to progressive sanctification. We must not only place our faith in Christ and what He did for us at Calvary, but we must maintain our faith in every capacity in Christ and what He has done for us at the Cross. What needs to be done in our hearts and lives cannot be done by the means of the flesh. It can only be done by the Holy Spirit, and He works exclusively within the parameters of the finished work of Christ.

HOW THE HOLY SPIRIT WORKS

Many Christians, if they think about the Holy Spirit at all, think that whatever He does is done automatically. Were that the case, there would never be a failure among Christians. The Holy Spirit would step in and stop the believer from going the wrong direction, but we know that's not the case, don't we?

The Holy Spirit doesn't demand much of us, but He does demand one thing, and on that He will not bend or move. He demands that our faith be exclusively in Christ and what Christ has done for us at the Cross.

Paul said again:

There is therefore now no condemnation (guilt) *to them which are in Christ Jesus* (refers back to Romans 6:3-5 and our being baptized into His death, which speaks of the crucifixion), *who walk not after the flesh* (depending on one's personal strength and ability or great religious efforts in order to overcome sin), *but after the Spirit* (the Holy Spirit works exclusively within the legal confines of the finished work of Christ; our faith in that finished work, i.e., 'the Cross,' guarantees the help of the Holy Spirit, which guarantees victory). *For the law* (that which we are about to give is a law of God, devised by the Godhead in eternity past [I Pet. 1:18-20]; this law, in fact, is 'God's prescribed order of victory') *of the Spirit* (Holy Spirit, i.e., 'the way the Spirit works') *of life* (all life comes from Christ but through the Holy Spirit [Jn. 16:13-14]) *in Christ Jesus* (anytime Paul uses this term or one of its derivatives, he is, without fail, referring to what Christ did at the Cross, which makes this 'life' possible) *has made me free* (given me total victory) *from the law of sin and death* (these are the two most powerful laws in the universe; the 'law of the Spirit of life in Christ Jesus' alone is stronger than the 'law of sin and death'; this means that if the believer attempts to live for God by any manner other than faith in Christ and the Cross, he is doomed to failure) (Rom. 8:1-2) (The Expositor's Study Bible).

WHAT IS FLESH?

Paul used this term *flesh* quite a number of times in his teaching. It refers to the motivation, education, ability, talent, self-will, willpower, etc., of the individual. In other words, it's what a human being can do. So, the Holy Spirit through Paul is telling us that we cannot do what we need to do, be what we need to be, function as we need to function, and have the victory that we must have, in other words, our sanctification, by means of the flesh. It cannot be done that way. It has to be done by way of the Holy Spirit, which is the way of the Cross (Rom. 8:5-10).

THE OVERCOMER

"He who overcomes shall inherit all things; and I will be his God, and he shall be My son" (Rev. 21:7).

The phrase, *"He who overcomes shall inherit all things,"* proclaims the requirement for inheritance. This is the fifth statement.

The message of our Lord to the seven churches of Asia is unequivocally clear regarding the necessity of being an overcomer. Considering that He repeats Himself seven times, we should understand how absolutely necessary is this requirement. Understanding that, surely it's incumbent upon us to desire to know exactly how we can guarantee the position of overcomer.

Please understand that this position of victory is required for all. There is no such thing as a believer who is such, but yet, does not fall into the category of being an overcomer. Now, we should think about that statement because, in effect, the Holy Spirit links salvation and the position of overcomer as one and the same.

Please allow me to be clearer: There is no such thing as a true believer who is not an overcomer. There are millions who claim to be believers, but who aren't overcomers, which, in effect, God labels as unbelievers. That's why Paul said, *"Examine yourselves, whether you be in the faith; prove your own selves. Know you not your own selves, how that Jesus Christ is in you, except you be reprobates?"* (II Cor. 13:5).

As is obvious in this passage, one is either in the faith, or else, he is a reprobate.

Reprobate in the Greek is *adokimos* and means, "unapproved, worthless, rejected, castaway."

So, how does one guarantee one's position as an overcomer?

In the first place, there is nothing we can do within our own strength, ability, or prowess that can make of us an overcomer. Any and all efforts of this nature constitute the person walking after the flesh, which God can never accept (Rom. 8:1, 8). Regrettably, if most Christians were told that they had to be an overcomer, which, incidentally, is seldom preached, they would automatically resort to the effort of attempting to be more religious, whatever that means.

HOW TO BE AN OVERCOMER!

The believer is an overcomer only in Christ. There is no other way. Actually, it is a simple way, and would remain so were it not for the self-will of Christians.

The believer is to understand that everything he is in Christ, everything he receives from the Lord, and every attribute of salvation, all, and in entirety, comes through what Jesus did at the Cross; consequently, the believer's faith must rest exclusively in the finished work of Christ.

God honors such faith, which, in fact, is the only thing He will honor (Rom 5:1-2; Eph. 2:8-9). Let us make the following statement, and then we will elaborate on it: Every person in the world who is truly born again is an overcomer. It's not something they will be, but it's something they presently are. Please understand that we are overcomers because of our faith in Christ and what Christ did at the Cross and not because of other things we do or don't do. When the word *overcomer* is mentioned, most believers start looking at themselves. We always find some things that are wrong, and, thereby, we judge ourselves as not quite being overcomers and that we have to try harder to, in fact, be overcomers.

That's the wrong way to look at the situation. Forget about yourself. Look exclusively to Christ and His Cross and keep your faith there, and that constitutes your being an overcomer.

When the believer places his faith exclusively in Christ and the Cross, and maintains it exclusively in Christ and the Cross, God marks him down as an overcomer simply because he is in Christ. If we try to bring this about by our own machinations, then we automatically fail. I'm an overcomer not because of what I have done or not done, but because of what my Lord has done for me at the Cross and my faith in that finished work.

Now that doesn't mean that God overlooks sin in any capacity. You must understand the only way that you are going to get victory over your weaknesses, your failures, or your sins, whatever they might be, is by you placing your faith exclusively in Christ and the Cross. Then the Holy Spirit can go to work in your life and make things as they ought to be. Once again, we're coming back to sanctification, with our condition being brought up to our position. Whatever is wrong with us, it is impossible for us to overcome it within our own strength and ability, and I don't care how consecrated we are as believers. It can be overcome only by the means that the Holy Spirit has given us, and that's by the means of the Cross.

That's why Paul said, *"For the preaching of the Cross is to them who perish foolishness; but unto us who are saved it is the power of God"* (I Cor. 1:18).

That's why Paul also said, *"For I determined not to know anything among you, save Jesus Christ, and Him crucified"* (I Cor. 2:2).

All of this is the reason that Satan fights the Cross to such an extent. He knows that all salvation is in the Cross even as all victory is in the Cross and the Cross alone. In fact, the Cross is the great dividing line between the true church and the apostate church.

In relationship to this, Paul also said, *"But God forbid that I should glory, save in the Cross of our Lord Jesus Christ, by whom the world is crucified unto me, and I unto the world"* (Gal. 6:14).

RELATIONSHIP

The phrase, *"And I will be his God, and he shall be My*

son," refers to the fact that we as true believers are definitely in Christ, and being in Christ means that we are a part of the family of God.

Paul also said:

"For you have not received the spirit of bondage again to fear; but you have received the Spirit of adoption (a work of the Holy Spirit), *whereby we cry, Abba, Father. The Spirit itself* (Himself) *bears witness with our spirit, that we are the children of God: And if children, then heirs* (we are in the family); *heirs of God, and joint-heirs with Christ; if so be that we suffer with Him, that we may be also glorified together"* (Rom. 8:15-17) (The Expositor's Study Bible).

To be frank, everything hinges on Christ and what He did at the Cross and our faith in that finished work. Let not the believer misunderstand this. This is the single most important thing that one can know.

The believer doesn't have to be a theologian. He doesn't even have to be a so-called faith giant. However, one thing he must do is understand his salvation and how it is obtained. As well, properly understanding salvation means that one properly understands sanctification also.

SALVATION AND SANCTIFICATION

Let us explain: In effect, salvation and sanctification are in a sense one and the same. In other words, the sinner is saved by simply believing in Christ and what Christ has done at the Cross. To be frank, he doesn't understand anything about it; he just simply believes. When this is done, he is instantly placed into the family of God, which Christ referred to as being *"born again"* (Jn. 3:3, 16).

After the believer comes to Christ, the Holy Spirit now takes up residence within the believer's life and is there for the purpose of guiding us *"into all truth"* (Jn. 16:13).

This *"all truth"* is wrapped up in the words, as given by Christ, *"He (the Holy Spirit) shall glorify Me"* (Jn. 16:14). This refers to what Christ has done for us at the Cross. In fact, the Holy Spirit works exclusively, as previously stated, within the parameters of the finished work of Christ, and by that, we speak of the atonement. The Holy Spirit doesn't work according to parameters that we lay down but always within the confines of the sacrifice of Christ. That is what makes everything possible!

So, the believer is to understand this and, thereby, anchor his faith in that great sacrifice, understanding that it is through this that all things are made possible. That's why Paul said, *"Christ sent me not to baptize, but to preach the gospel: not with wisdom of* (enticing) *words, lest the Cross of Christ should be made of none effect"* (I Cor. 1:17).

THE CROSS

The apostle wasn't belittling water baptism or any other or-dinance of the church. In fact, these things are very, very im-portant, but only in their proper place. It is through the Cross that all victory comes and not through water baptism, the Lord's Supper, speaking with other tongues, confessing certain

Scriptures, or anything else we might name of this nature.

As stated, all of these things we've named, and many we haven't named, are very important; however, they are important in their own place and right. We are to never major in these things but only in the Cross. When we major in the Cross, understanding what the Cross afforded us, the Holy Spirit, who works exclusively within the parameters of the Cross, can do great and mighty things within our hearts and lives (Rom. 8:1-11, I Cor. 2:2, 5).

So, to have a proper relationship with God, we must understand that we are sons only in respect to what Christ has done for us at the Cross and our faith in that finished work. It is all in Christ!

John also said, *"This is the victory that overcomes the world, even our faith"* (I Jn. 5:4). So, there you have the meaning of the word *overcomer*.

THE FEARFUL AND UNBELIEVING

"But the fearful, and unbelieving, and the abominable, and murderers, and whoremongers, and sorcerers, and idolaters, and all liars, shall have their part in the lake which burns with fire and brimstone: which is the second death" (Rev. 21:8).

Revelation 21:8 proclaims two facts:

1. The faithless will be eternally lost.
2. If the gospel believed doesn't change the person, then it's not a true gospel.

All of this corresponds with the *"works of the flesh,"* as outlined in Galatians 5:19-21.

"Fearful and unbelieving" are, in a sense, linked together. What does it mean?

Paul plainly told us that there is an offense linked to the Cross (Gal. 5:11). Consequently, this same verse proclaims the fact that for those who place their faith and trust in Christ and what He has done at the Cross, persecution will definitely follow. As Paul put it, persecution will come from within the church.

If one pulls aside all the cover and veneer, one finds that the Cross, even as we've already stated, is the dividing line. That's where the rubber meets the road, so to speak. You have those in the church who look to other things and then the few who look to Christ and the Cross. There is a war going on between the two exactly as the one between Cain and Abel. No, the war was not begun by Abel, but rather by Cain (Gen., Chpt. 4); neither is this present war instigated by true believers. However, those who look to things other than the Cross will definitely wage war. They not only oppose the Cross, but they also feel that they must stop the voices of all who trust in Christ and the Cross. In fact, this is where the great war is and has always been.

There are millions who fear the wrath of those who hold up their works religion, which means they simply will not buck the tide. Their fear puts them in the place of unbelief, which puts them in the place of the lake of fire.

Then we have the abominable, the murderers, the whoremongers, etc. This constitutes the group who claims that one can have salvation and sin at the same time. The church world is full of this type also.

CHANGE

The gospel of Jesus Christ changes men. In fact, if there is
no change wrought in one's life, despite the profession, the individual simply is not saved. This is not meant to attempt to teach
sinless perfection, for the Bible doesn't teach such; however,
the Bible definitely does teach that sin will not have dominion
over us (Rom. 6:14). So, for one to claim salvation and at the
same time continue on in an ungodly lifestyle with no effort to
change, such a one is only fooling oneself. Regrettably, there are
millions who fall into this category!

Jesus said:

> *Not everyone who says unto Me, Lord, Lord, shall enter
> into the kingdom of heaven* (the repetition of the word
> 'Lord' expresses astonishment, as if to say: 'Are we to be
> disowned?'); *but he who does the will of my Father which
> is in heaven* (what is the will of the Father? Verse 24 tells
> us). *Many will say to Me in that day, Lord, Lord, have
> we not prophesied in Your name? and in Your name have
> cast out devils* (demons)? *and in Your name done many
> wonderful works?* (These things are not the criteria, but
> rather faith in Christ and what Christ has done for us at the
> Cross [Eph. 2:8-9, 13-18]. The Word of God alone is to be
> the judge of doctrine.) *And then will I profess unto them,
> I never knew you* (again we say, the criteria alone is Christ
> and Him crucified [I Cor. 1:23]): *depart from Me, you
> who work iniquity* (we have access to God only through
> Christ, and access to Christ only through the Cross, and

access to the Cross only through a denial of self [Lk. 9:23];
any other message is judged by God as 'iniquity' and cannot be a part of Christ [I Cor. 1:17]) (Mat. 7:21-23) (The
Expositor's Bible).

Jesus went on to say, *"Therefore whosoever hears these sayings of Mine, and does them, I will liken him unto a wise man,
which built his house upon a rock* (the 'rock' is Christ Jesus,
and the foundation is the Cross [Gal. 1:8-9])*"* (Mat. 7:24).

FIRE AND BRIMSTONE

In Revelation 21:8, the phrase, *"shall have their part
in the lake which burns with fire and brimstone: which is
the second death,"* proclaims the eternal destiny of Christ-
rejecters. The entirety of verse 8 is the seventh statement made
by the Lord to John. The seven statements are as follows:

1. I make all things new.
2. These words are true and faithful.
3. I am the beginning and the end.
4. He who is athirst, I will give the fountain of the water
   of life freely.
5. The overcomer will inherit all things.
6. I will be his God, and he shall be My son.
7. The eternal destiny of Christ-rejecters will be the
   lake which burns with fire and brimstone. Incidentally, eternal hell, which will be the eternal destina-
   tion for all Christ-rejecters, is the second death. As
   someone has well said, "There is nothing worse than
   a false way of salvation."

Sing the wondrous love of Jesus
Sing His mercy and His grace:
In the mansions bright and blessed
He'll prepare for us a place.

While we walk the pilgrim pathway
Clouds will overspread the sky,
But when traveling days are over,
Not a shadow, not a sigh.

Let us then be true and faithful,
Trusting, serving every day;
Just one glimpse of Him in glory
Will the toils of life repay.

Onward to the prize before us!
Soon His beauty we'll behold;
Soon the pearly gates will open.
We shall tread the streets of gold.

When we all get to heaven,
What a day of rejoicing that will be!
When we all see Jesus,
We'll sing and shout the victory.

THE NEW JERUSALEM

CHAPTER 2

THE LAMB'S WIFE

THE LAMB'S WIFE

"AND THERE CAME UNTO me one of the seven angels which had the seven vials full of the seven last plagues, and talked with me, saying, Come hither, I will show you the bride, the Lamb's wife" (Rev. 21:9).

THE ANGEL

The passage is self-explanatory. This is one of the seven angels who had one of the seven vials of wrath, who had shown to John the scarlet-clad harlot, the great and guilty Babylon (Rev., Chpt. 15). One of these seven, and it is possible that it was the same one, now showed John the bride of the Lamb, the new and holy Jerusalem. What a contrast! The former writes "finished," while the latter writes "beginning."

THE BRIDE

The phrase, *"saying, Come hither* (here), *I will show you the bride, the Lamb's wife,"* tells us several things:

- Some have concluded the Lamb's wife to be the church alone; however, that is incorrect. The Lamb's wife includes every single person who has ever been saved, all the way from Abel to the last one who comes to Christ during the great tribulation. No doubt, it will also include all who will give their hearts to Christ during the kingdom age. In other words, none will be excluded. Do we honestly think that the great faith worthies, as listed in Hebrews, Chapter 11, who are all Old Testament saints, are to be excluded? Of course not!

- There is only one kind of faith as it regards salvation, and that's faith in Christ, and that goes for faith on either side of the Cross. That God honors, and that alone God honors.

- By the angel referring to Christ here as *"the Lamb,"* it proclaims the fact of Calvary and faith in that finished work. The idea is that every single person who has ever been saved—and that again goes all the way back to the beginning—has been saved because of what Christ did at the Cross and his faith in that great sacrifice. In fact, all of the sacrifices of the Old Testament, whether before the law of Moses or during the time of the law of Moses, represented Christ and what He would do regarding the giving of Himself as the great ransom, i.e., the sacrifice.

- The whole of the great plan of God as it regards redemption is anchored squarely in Christ and Him crucified, which is proven by the use, as stated, of the word *Lamb*.

There isn't but one salvation, and that is by faith in Christ and what He did at the Cross. Peter said, *"Neither is there salvation in any other: for there is none other name under heaven given among men, whereby we must be saved"* (Acts 4:12).

I remind the reader that Peter, at this particular time in Jerusalem, was speaking altogether to Jews. So, the idea that there is one type of salvation for Jews and another for Gentiles holds no scriptural validity whatsoever. So, the Lamb's wife consists of every single person who has ever trusted Christ in the history of humanity.

IN THE SPIRIT

"And he carried me away in the Spirit to a great and high mountain, and showed me that great city, the holy Jerusalem, descending out of heaven from God" (Rev. 21:10).

The phrase, *"And he carried me away in the Spirit to a great and high mountain,"* refers to the apostle seeing all of this in a vision. The Spirit referred to here is the Holy Spirit. In the original text, the definite article "the" is in front of the word *Spirit,* signifying that it is the Holy Spirit, which means that it should have been capitalized by the translators. It is the same as when he said, *"I was in the Spirit on the Lord's day, and heard behind me a great voice"* (Rev. 1:10).

All believers have the Holy Spirit, but only some are baptized with the Spirit. All who are baptized with the Holy Spirit will speak with other tongues as the Spirit of God gives the utterance (Acts 2:4; 10:44-48; 19:1-7). In fact, none of this that John describes would be possible without the moving and operation of the Holy Spirit. Every single thing that the believer receives that is truly from God is all carried out by the Holy Spirit in one way or the other.

THE MODERN CHURCH

The problem with the modern church is that it is little *led* by the Spirit and is, thereby, very little *in* the Spirit. This means that whatever is done, although it may be religious, it will actually serve no purpose for God. In fact, that is the problem with most churches. They are veritable beehives of activity, but all of it is man-devised. In fact, and I say this sadly, most that go under the name "church" aren't even recognized by God as such.

Jesus told the church at Ephesus, *"Remember therefore from where you have fallen, and repent, and do the first works; or else I will come unto you quickly, and will remove your candlestick* (lampstand) *out of his place, except you repent"* (Rev. 2:5).

The candlestick represents light, which symbolizes the church. To be sure, if it's not functioning according to what the Holy Spirit desires, its candlestick will be removed. This means that as far as the Lord is concerned, it's no longer a church. He then said, *"He who has an ear, let him hear what the Spirit says unto the churches"* (Rev. 2:7).

If the Word of God is not properly preached within the church, then the Word of God is not truly being preached. To properly preach means to preach without fear, favoritism, or compromise, which means to preach the Cross.

HOW MANY CHURCHES PRESENTLY
ARE PREACHING THE CROSS?

The churches that are actually preaching the Cross are so few as to be almost nonexistent; however, what few there are, they actually represent that which is being done for God in this world. This means that those not preaching the Cross are, in effect, doing nothing for the Lord. They may be involved in great religious activity, but it may even be probable that they are doing much harm.

Let's go back to a previous statement: If what we do is not born of the Spirit—activated by the Spirit, empowered by the Spirit, led by the Spirit, and anointed by the Spirit—then it's not of God. Irrespective of how religious it might be, it will serve no purpose whatsoever.

In fact, it's impossible to have the moving and operation of the Holy Spirit without one's faith being anchored in the Cross. Total trust in the sacrifice of Christ shows that one is dependent totally upon Christ. The Holy Spirit will always honor this trust because it provides a fertile field in which He can work. Trust in other things builds self-righteousness, but the Holy Spirit cannot function in such an atmosphere.

THE HOLY JERUSALEM

In Revelation 21:10, the phrase, *"And showed me that great city, the holy Jerusalem, descending out of heaven from God,"* presents a vision of the New Jerusalem, which John will proceed to describe minutely. John saw it descending, meaning that it is coming down to earth. In fact, the day is coming, which will be after God has made the new heaven and new earth, when the Lord will change His headquarters from heaven to earth.

The great city of Revelation, Chapter 17, is man's; this one is God's. It is called *"the bride, the Lamb's wife"* because of those who inhabit it. The Lamb's wife is to live in a golden city whose builder and maker is God.

As well, this is a literal city and not something that is symbolic, and it definitely isn't a metaphor. It is a great city, and it is called *"the holy Jerusalem."* In fact, it is so literal that we are given the dimensions in almost every capacity as it regards this city—the eternal abode of the redeemed.

IN CHRIST

As we go forward with our study, we should contemplate very carefully all that is said because this is the place where you will abide forever and forever, that is, if you are born again. This is your eternal home! To be sure, it is of such grandeur as to defy all description. Understanding that, how could we be worthy of such grace and glory?

The facts are that within ourselves, we aren't worthy and, in fact, cannot be worthy; however, because we are the Lamb's wife, that fact alone has made us worthy. To be in Christ is to be everything. Once again, let us emphasize that all of this—the beauty, the glory, the wonder, the rapture, the grandeur—all and without exception, and above all, our part in this eternal abode, is made possible exclusively by what Jesus did at the Cross.

No wonder Paul wrote, quoting Isaiah:

"But as it is written, Eye has not seen, nor ear heard, neither have entered into the heart of man, the things which God has prepared for them who love Him. But God has revealed them unto us by His Spirit: for the Spirit searches all things, yes, the deep things of God" (I Cor. 2:9-10; Isa. 64:4).

THE GLORY OF GOD

"Having the glory of God: and her light was like unto a stone most precious, even like a jasper stone, clear as crystal" (Rev. 21:11).

The phrase, *"Having the glory of God,"* is that which makes the city what it is. Everything else is wonderful, but it is the glory of God that gives it the light and luster that makes it different than any city that has ever existed.

While the Jerusalem of the millennial reign will be great and wonderful because Jesus will rule from this particular place, still, as grand and glorious as that city might be, God will not think enough of it for it to be preserved. It will be destroyed completely in the renovation of the heaven and the earth.

Of the millennial Jerusalem, we are told that the *"glory of the LORD filled the house,"* referring to the temple, but it mentions nothing about the city itself (Ezek. 43:2, 4-5). Of the New Jerusalem, the entirety of the city will be filled with the glory of God.

Occasionally (some more often than others), we sense the glory of God on our person. It is a feeling of unimagined presence, for, in reality, it is the presence of God.

Many times I have gone to prayer and have been tremendously troubled in my spirit. The problems, whatever they might have been, were pressing, and there seemed to be no solution; however, countless times, the Spirit of God in the realm of the glory of God would come upon me. When this would happen, the spirit of oppression would instantly leave, and euphoria would fill my heart to such an extent as to defy all description.

That is the glory of God and how privileged we are to sense it even at all; however, that which is to come will not be upon us merely on occasion, but will be perpetual. In other words, we will live in this glory time without end, which literally staggers the imagination. If you are truly saved, then you know what I'm talking about because you have momentarily sensed that glory yourself. Now, think of living in that forever and forever!

HER LIGHT

In Revelation 21:11 the phrase, *"And her light was like unto a stone most precious, even like a jasper stone, clear as crystal,"* presents the radiance of God's glory. Verse 23 says, *"For the glory of God did lighten it, and the Lamb is the light thereof."*

Considering that this light is like a jasper stone, more than likely that is what the angel told him, for it is doubtful that John would have had that much knowledge of precious stones. This would mean that it is a prism of light, which refers to colors constantly changing, which would be indescribably beautiful. And yet, each color of light diminishes not at all the crystal clarity of light. It is abundant in color, for a jasper stone is of that manner, but yet, it is clear as crystal, meaning that sight is not impeded at all.

We struggle in our efforts to explain what John saw, and no matter how close we might think we come to a proper explanation, the truth is, we aren't close at all! In even attempting to explain these descriptions, I can sense the presence of God. So, what will it really be like when at long last, we actually stand in this city, even as all born-again believers shall?

A WALL

"And had a wall great and high, and had twelve gates, and at the gates twelve angels, and names written thereon, which are the names of the twelve tribes of the children of Israel" (Rev. 21:12).

The phrase, *"And had a wall great and high,"* presents that which is definitely decorative, as we shall see, but also carries a spiritual connotation, which we shall also see.

This wall will be 216 feet high, counting 18 inches to the cubit (Rev. 21:17). As well, we will find that the city has 12 gates, three on each side, and at each gate, there stands an angel. Also, on the gates are the names of the 12 tribes of the children of Israel.

TWELVE GATES

The phrase, *"And had twelve gates,"* signifies three gates on the north, three gates on the south, three gates on the east, and three gates on the west. The gates on each side will be about 500 miles distance from each other.

Twelve is the number of God's government; consequently, the government of God will rule this city, which means there will be perfect government in every respect.

For there to be perfect government, there must be perfect obedience; however, considering that perfect obedience will come from perfection, obedience will not be a chore at all but will be the norm. We are speaking of every saint of God, who definitely will then be perfect. To be sure, there will be no desire for anything other than that which adds to the glory of God.

THE GOVERNMENT OF GOD

Down through the ages, because of man's lost condition, his problem has ever been with the government of God. In fact, that is the greatest problem with the church as well.

In the book of Acts and the Epistles, we are given by the Holy Spirit the government that the Lord intends and a description of how it is to be carried out. Unfortunately, religious men are seldom satisfied with God's government and, thereby, set out to change it.

Sometime back, one of the large Pentecostal denominations changed one of its rulings. To be frank, it's something that should have never been instituted to begin with. However, they had subscribed to this unscriptural ruling ever since 1914.

As should be obvious, if it was scriptural, how could they change it? Well, of course, they have changed it because it was not scriptural. Unfortunately, the government of this particular denomination is not scriptural in many aspects. It's because men make rules that have no scriptural foundation. That is the bane of the church and, in fact, has always been the bane of the church.

TWELVE ANGELS

The phrase, *"And at the gates twelve angels,"* proclaims the fact of the glory of the city and, as well, the glory of God's government.

Whether the same angels will remain there forever, we aren't told, but it is likely that there will be different angels, but with the place and position at each gate always occupied.

The Scriptures do provide some insight regarding angels:

- All angels were created by God (Jn. 1:3). They were created without number, possibly many billions. They were all created at the same time, meaning that there has never been such a thing as a baby angel. They were created fully mature. How do we know that? We know that simply because there is no record in the Bible of a baby angel or anything of such nature.

- While all angels were created at the same time, which

means sometime in eternity past, there are different ranks regarding their place and position. In Jude
1:9, Michael is listed as an archangel, which seems to
be the highest rank. And yet, it is said of the mighty
angel Gabriel that he *"stands in the presence of God"*
(Lk. 1:19). There could be precious little, if anything,
higher than that. Then, at the same time, when Luci-
fer was created by God, there is some evidence that he
was created with greater wisdom than any other angel
and, as well, with greater beauty (Ezek. 28:12). All of
this means that it's possible that before his fall, Luci-
fer was the most powerful angel created by God. He
led a revolution against God sometime in eternity past
and drew with him about one-third of the angelic host,
whatever that number may have been (Rev. 12:3-4).

- There is coming a time, which will be immediately
after the second coming of our Lord, when Satan,
along with all demon spirits and fallen angels, will be
put into the bottomless pit. There they will be locked
up for the duration of the kingdom age, which will be a
thousand years (Rev. 20:1-3). Then, at the end of that
time, they will be loosed for a short period of time and
will then be cast into the lake of fire where they will be
forever and forever (Rev. 20:7-10).

THE TWELVE TRIBES

The phrase, *"And names written thereon, which are*

the names of the twelve tribes of the children of Israel," proclaims the fact that the Lamb's wife is made up of every single believer, whether on the other side of the Cross or this side of the Cross. Every gate will have the name of one of the 12 tribes.

As well, this tells us how precious to the heart of God is Israel, and it is precious because of Israel's faith. Also, this proclaims the fact that Israel will experience a great restoration, to which we have already addressed ourselves. She will yet function as she should function and as God always intended.

The troubles and the problems have been many, with her not even recognizing the Lamb when He came into her midst. And then, agony upon agonies, she crucified the Lamb, which brought her untold suffering and sorrow.

However, God is never defeated. Ultimately, He will bring her back. It will not be an easy task, and, in fact, this trying hour called *"the time of Jacob's trouble"* is just ahead of us. Nonetheless, it will succeed in what it is designed to do—bring Israel back to God (Jer. 30:7).

THE GATES

"On the east three gates; on the north three gates; on the south three gates; and on the west three gates" (Rev. 21:13).

As previously stated, there are 12 gates, three to a side. Three gates on each side proclaims the fact of the Trinity—the Father, the Son, and the Holy Spirit.

Having three gates on each side also proclaims the fact that salvation is the same for all.

THE EAST

The phrase, *"On the east three gates,"* probably means these gates will have the names Joseph, Benjamin, and Dan.

THE NORTH

The phrase, *"On the north three gates,"* probably means these gates will have the names Reuben, Judah, and Levi.

THE SOUTH

The phrase, *"On the south three gates,"* probably means these gates will have the names Simeon, Issachar, and Zebulun.

THE WEST

The phrase, *"And on the west three gates,"* probably means these gates will have the names Gad, Asher, and Naphtali.

The Scripture doesn't say here, but the names of the 12 tribes of Israel that are inscribed on the gates of the heavenly city, and the order of their placement on each side, are probably the same as given in the description by Ezekiel concerning the millennial temple of the Jerusalem of that day (Ezek. 48:31-34). We may wonder why the names of the 12 tribes of Israel are inscribed on the gates of this celestial city, considering that this will be forever and forever.

The reason goes back to Abraham. It was to the Patriarch that the great plan of salvation was given as it regarded justification by faith (Gen. 15:6). In order for this plan to be brought to fruition, a people would have to be raised up who would have faith in Jehovah. Incidentally, those people came from the loins of Abraham and the womb of Sarah. They were called Israelites, and to them was given the Word of God. As well, they would serve as the womb of the Messiah. All of this had to be if salvation was to come to the world. This is why Jesus said to the woman at Jacob's well, *"Salvation is of the Jews"* (Jn. 4:22). Consequently, Christ Himself was of Jewish ancestry. As well, not only are all the names on the gates Jewish, but the twelve apostles, whose names are on the 12 foundations, are Jewish also.

GENTILES

Paul said that the Gentiles were grafted into the tree of Israel (Rom. 11:17). As it regards salvation, the great plan of God includes the entirety of mankind; however, it was brought into the world by the Jews, and that must not be forgotten. In fact, the New Jerusalem guarantees that it will not be forgotten. However, with the names of the 12 tribes on the gates and the names of the apostles on the foundations, both the Old and New Testaments are held up in their entirety as the Word of God. Jesus Christ, who is the light of this city, is the fulfillment of the entirety of the Word.

The presence of angels at each gate proclaims that this is God's city, while the 12 tribes and the twelve apostles emphasize the fact that the city is for the Lamb's wife, which consists of all the redeemed who have ever lived.

TWELVE FOUNDATIONS

"And the wall of the city had twelve foundations, and in them the names of the twelve apostles of the Lamb" (Rev. 21:14).

The phrase, *"And the wall of the city had twelve foundations,"* portrays the following facts:

- The way of salvation was originally shown to the Jews, hence, the gates and the names of the 12 tribes inscribed on those gates; however, the foundation of the salvation message was not really given until after the Cross, because it could not be given until after the Cross.

- One might say that both the Old and New Testament church are represented in the appearance of the city, but the work of the apostles receives its special recognition. It is on their teaching and witness for Christ that the great spiritual Jerusalem is built. There is a complete harmony of thought here between Paul and John. Paul described the church as built upon the foundation of the apostles and prophets (described here by John), with Jesus Christ Himself being the chief cornerstone (Eph. 2:20). We may compare the same illustration used by our Lord (Mat. 16:18) and afterward by Peter (I Pet. 2:4-6).

- Concerning the foundations, once again, the number

12 is used, signifying the government of God. As the entrance to the city by the 12 gates proclaims the perfect government of entrance, the 12 foundations on which the city rests proclaim the fact that this city rests upon the foundation of a perfect government.

THE TWELVE APOSTLES

The phrase, *"And in them the names of the twelve apostles of the Lamb,"* tells us two things:

1. The gates could not be opened unless the foundation was secure.
2. The foundation of the salvation message, which is the message of redemption, is based 100 percent upon Christ. Until Christ came and died on the Cross, which the word *Lamb* represents, the salvation message was incomplete.

The first use of the word *Lamb* given to us in Verse 9 has to do with redemption. The second use found in the verse of our study has to do with the foundation of redemption, which is the Cross.

Make no mistake about it, the Holy Spirit had John to use the word *Lamb* for a specific reason. It was to proclaim to us that all of the greatness and glory portrayed in Chapters 21 and 22, which, incidentally, will be eternal, are made possible by Jesus and what He did at the Cross. The word *Lamb* goes back to the proclamation of John the Baptist, *"Behold the Lamb of God, which takes away the sin of the world"*

(Jn. 1:29). He was to be and, in fact, is the fulfillment of the great prophecy given by Isaiah in Chapter 53 of his book.

THE PROPHET

"And he who talked with me had a golden reed to mea-sure the city, and the gates thereof, and the wall thereof" (Rev. 21:15).

The phrase, *"And he who talked with me,"* proclaims one different than the angel of Verse 9. The idea seems to be that one of the seven angels that had the seven vials had shown John the New Jerusalem as it regarded some of its particulars.

And now, someone else began to talk with John, who, incidentally, identified himself as a prophet in Revelation 22:9, but he looked so much like an angel, or perhaps even like our Lord, that John proceeded to worship him. He was stopped and told to worship God.

This seems to be the second time that John did this (Rev. 19:10).

Why would the apostle do this and, in fact, make the same mistake twice?

Some have attempted to ascribe this to the incurable idolatry of the human heart. In fact, concerning this very thing, Williams said, "That the apostle John should have twice so acted is a proof of the incurable religious blindness of the natural mind, and of its idolatrous bent."

Personally, I don't think that was John's problem. If it is to be noticed, both times the apostle did this, and I speak of the attempt to worship the one with whom he was speaking, it was a man and not an angel.

It is my thought that the redeemed in glory will look so much like Christ that it will be difficult to tell the difference. In fact, John had written a short time earlier: *"Beloved, now are we the sons of God, and it does not yet appear what we shall be: but we know that, when He shall appear, we shall be like Him; for we shall see Him as He is"* (I Jn. 3:2).

MEASUREMENTS

The phrase, *"Had a golden reed to measure the city, and the gates thereof, and the wall thereof,"* will be found to be in multiples of 12.

The measuring is done for a reason. It reveals the perfection, fulfillment, and completion of all of God's purposes for His redeemed people. As 12 is God's number for government, and perfect government at that, we will find here that the government in every capacity and in every way is the epitome of perfection. It means that there is nothing lacking in this salvation. What Jesus did at the Cross, symbolized by the use of the word *Lamb*, was truly a finished work.

When John closed out the book of Revelation, he said:

"For I testify unto every man who hears the words of the prophecy of this book, if any man shall add unto these things, God shall add unto him the plagues that are written in this book: And if any man shall take away from the words of the book of this prophecy, God shall take away his part out of

the book of life, and out of the holy city, and from the things which are written in this book" (Rev. 22:18-19).

In effect, the Holy Spirit through the apostle is saying that man is not to take from the Cross or add to the Cross.

We know this was a finished work, as well, from the 28 times the word *Lamb* is used in the book of Revelation regarding Christ. Of course, the title or word *Lamb* portrays what Christ did at the Cross.

Also, *Lamb* is used seven times in the last two chapters, even though all things there are perfection, with sin and Satan completely done away with. As we've already stated, this name is used with frequency in order that all know and understand that the greatness and glory described here was all brought about by what Jesus did at the Cross. As well, *Lamb* is mentioned seven times to show that the work of the Cross was perfect and it, therefore, furnishes a perfect product.

FOURSQUARE

"And the city lies foursquare, and the length is as large as the breadth: and he measured the city with the reed, twelve thousand furlongs. The length and the breadth and the height of it are equal" (Rev. 21:16).

The furlongs mentioned in Verse 16 translate into about 1,500 miles per side. As is obvious, we have here the multiples of 12.

LENGTH, WIDTH, AND HEIGHT

The phrase, *"The length and the breadth and the height*

of it are equal," presents astounding dimensions.

The size of this city is, of course, unlike anything the world has previously known. If we set it down in the United States on the western side, it would reach approximately from Vancouver, British Columbia, Canada, to Los Angeles, California. That is the distance from north to south. Going east, it would reach Dallas, Texas, on the southeastern corner and Minneapolis, Minnesota, on the northeastern corner. So, we have a space here that's a little over half of the United States.

This is not to mean that this is where the city will be, but we use these numbers to give you an idea of the size of the city.

Its occupants will consist not only of all those who have believed in God and in Christ (Jn. 14:1), but, also, all of the infants and little children who have died before they reached the age of accountability. Of course, they will not remain infants or little children, as should be obvious, because all there will be perfect, which speaks of maturity, etc.

Concerning the size of this city, no wonder Jesus said:

"In My Father's house are many mansions: if it were not so, I would have told you. I go to prepare a place for you. And if I go and prepare a place for you, I will come again, and receive you unto Myself; that where I am, there you may be also" (Jn. 14:2-3).

THE HEIGHT

If the length and the width of this city are not enough, we are also told that the height is the same as the length and the width, which means that the city is also 1,500 miles high.

Some have claimed that it's built in the shape of a pyramid, and others, that it is a perfect cube. From the way the description is given, more than likely the pyramid type of structure is correct. This means that its top stone would be some 1,500 miles above its base.

This vast mountain will be made of transparent gold. It will, in a sense, be the garden of Eden restored, but on a far grander scale. The garden of Eden was possibly a pyramid. The Tower of Babel was a pyramid and was man's effort to restore the garden of Eden and to construct a home that would be at once a city and a temple.

The pyramids of Egypt, Mexico, and other lands evidence this thirst of fallen man for a happiness that has been lost (Williams).

All of this proclaims the fact of a dimension beyond anything we now presently know. This speaks of travel, living conditions, and atmospheric conditions, which will totally change, with everything then being different than it is now.

A little bit above 10,000 feet is about the limit that people presently can live as it regards mountains, etc. To be sure, man can maybe exist a little higher than that without added oxygen; however, to live comfortably, one might say, not much above 10,000 feet would be the limit. In other words, it is not much above two miles high.

However, this city reaches 1,500 miles high, which means that the atmosphere up to the height, and perhaps even beyond, will be comfortable and livable.

OTHER CITIES?

We would wonder, would we not, if there will be other cities on the new earth that is to be, especially considering the size of this city?

To properly understand the size of this city, if we factor in the height, we are faced with a city larger than the entirety of the surface of this earth.

What exactly there will be, we aren't told; however, I don't think there will be a need, or even a desire, for other huge cities, especially considering the glory of the New Jerusalem. But yet, there will, no doubt, be thousands of small towns and villages all over the world.

THE HEIGHT OF THE WALL

"And he measured the wall thereof, an hundred and forty and four cubits, according to the measure of a man, that is, of the angel" (Rev. 21:17).

The phrase, *"And he measured the wall thereof, an hundred and forty and four cubits,"* translates into about 216 feet, that is, if we are using 18 inches to the cubit. Once again we come back to the multiples of 12.

Twelve times 12 is 144. As we shall see, the wall is built strictly for ornamentation. As well, its 12 times 12 height regarding cubits is once again a representation of perfect government, especially considering that it rests upon 12 foundations.

THE MEASURE

The phrase, *"According to the measure of a man, that is,*

of the angel," refers to Revelation 22:9, presenting the fact that this is a man speaking to John, even a prophet, but who looks like an angel.

Man's measurement is now finally the same as that of God's. We speak of righteousness. I think this is what the Holy Spirit is conveying here. Outside of Christ, it is impossible for man to measure up. Only with Christ can the measurement be that which God demands.

THE WALL IS OF JASPER

"And the building of the wall of it was of jasper: and the city was pure gold, like unto clear glass" (Rev. 21:18).

The phrase, *"And the building of the wall of it was of jasper,"* presents a precious stone of several colors. As the glory of God shines upon these colors, they are constantly changing. God must love color, and to be sure, this wall, some 216 feet high and some 6,000 miles in length, is, as would be obvious, totally unlike any other wall the world has ever known. It will be so beautiful as to be beyond description. How is it possible to describe a structure with colors constantly changing? Where will the Lord get that much jasper?

We must remember that this is a new earth!

PURE GOLD

The phrase, *"And the city was pure gold, like unto clear glass,"* takes us beyond imagination and beyond comprehension!

Many may ask, "Is all of this meant to be literal, or is it merely symbolic?"

It should be obvious that it is literal. That which is merely symbolic is never described in such detail. No, this is a literal city, and its description is literal; it will be exactly as the Word of God says that it will be.

Gold is the most beautiful metal there is. When we consider that it is pure gold, which means that it has no alloy, it will be beautiful beyond compare. As well, I'm told that such is slightly soft to the touch. We must also consider that it is transparent, but yet, with substance.

Read this chapter and believe it literally as God expects you to do, for it is a description of your literal future home, that is, if you are saved.

If we doubt the veracity of this that we are reading in Chapter 21, then we at the same time are doubting the ability of God. Why is it so hard for some to believe that God is able to do all things, in fact, that He is almighty?

This problem of doubt and unbelief was generated by the fall. It is a part of the sin nature, which is the proclivity of man to believe something that is untrue and disbelieve that which is true.

GARNISHED WITH PRECIOUS STONES

"And the foundations of the wall of the city were garnished with all manner of precious stones. The first foundation was jasper; the second, sapphire; the third, a chalcedony; the

fourth, an emerald; the fifth, sardonyx; the sixth, sardius; the seventh, chrysolite; the eighth, beryl; the ninth, a topaz; the tenth, a chrysoprasus; the eleventh, a jacinth; the twelfth, an amethyst" (Rev. 21:19-20).

The phrase, *"And the foundations of the wall of the city were garnished with all manner of precious stones,"* describes beauty upon beauty.

We are told that the walls are made of jasper, but we aren't told exactly what constitutes the substance of the foundations. Whatever it is, it, no doubt, is made to cause the beauty of the precious stones to stand out.

Foundations are normally under the ground, therefore, not seen, consequently, with no efforts made toward beauty; however, it seems that these 12 foundations are above the ground, with perhaps the first foundation extending partly in the ground down to bedrock. But again, quite possibly these foundations will have no similarity whatsoever to that of which we are normally accustomed. In other words, they could very well rest on the power of God and not at all on bedrock.

In the first place, there are 12 of these foundations, which seem to have a far greater spiritual value than material. As well, even as is overly obvious, the beauty is far more emphasized than anything else.

VARIETY OF PRECIOUS STONES

The phrase, *"The first foundation was jasper,"* is the same as the wall. This jasper has a greenish hue but is clear as crystal. The second is sapphire, which is blue. The third is a chalcedony, which is a greenish sort of emerald. The fourth is an emerald, which is bright green. The fifth is sardonyx, which is red and white. The sixth is sardius, which is a bright red. The seventh is chrysolite, which is a golden yellow. The eighth is beryl, which is bluish green. The ninth is a topaz, which is yellowish green. The tenth is a chrysoprasus, which is apple-green. The eleventh is a jacinth, which is blue. The twelfth is an amethyst, which is violet and purple.

Beginning from the last color mentioned, a marked similarity can be seen with seven prismatic colors—violet, indigo, blue, green, yellow, orange, and red. As stated, the first jasper is identical with the color of the wall above, and there can be no doubt but that the colors blend harmoniously with the wall of jasper, the first mentioned.

With this blended harmony of color, the foundation stones will encircle the heavenly city as with a rainbow belt. The light of the heavenly city will shine with hues that betoken the advent of the morning. The varying tints will glow like pledges of a dayspring from on high.

PRAISE UPON PRAISES

Oh, dear saint, can you not sense the presence of God even as we read of the description of this eternal abode of the redeemed? Once again, hear the words of Christ said so simply:

"Let not your heart be troubled: you believe in God,

*believe also in Me. In My Father's house are many mansions:
if it were not so, I would have told you. I go to prepare a place
for you"* (Jn. 14:1-2).

However, in a sense, let the reader understand that all of
this—the beauty, the glory, the grandeur, even that which is
indescribable—is all and without exception built upon the
precious, shed blood of our Lord and Saviour, Jesus Christ.
The preparing of this glorious place, this celestial city, this
New Jerusalem, holds no difficulty for God Almighty; however, that which made it possible for the redeemed to live
eternally in this great and glorious city is of such price as to
beggar description—the precious blood of Christ. This is
made obvious by the repetitive use of the word *Lamb* as it
refers to Christ.

Beyond imagination is the flooding of color in that incom-
parable city. All of these stones named here are exquisite in
color.

What beauty! What color! What loveliness! What grandeur! However, there is more to come.

PEARLS

*"And the twelve gates were twelve pearls; every several
gate was of one pearl: and the street of the city was pure gold,
as it were transparent glass"* (Rev. 21:21).

The phrase, *"And the twelve gates were twelve pearls,"*
probably means that each gate, which is about 216 feet high, is
made of untold thousands of pearls.

Criswell says: "There is a sermon in the fact that the gates are pearl. Heaven is entered through suffering and travail, through redemption and blood, through the agony of the Cross. A pearl is a jewel made by a little animal that is wounded. Without the wound, the pearl is never formed. We enter heaven through gates of pearl."

As well, the pearl is the only precious stone that the art and skill of man cannot improve. The tools of the craftsman and artificer may give fresh luster to the emerald and the sapphire, but he must lift no tool upon the pearl. So is it with the truth, which sets men free (Jn. 8:32; I Cor. 3:10). Through truth, and Him who is truth, we enter the city.

ONE PEARL

The phrase, *"Every several gate was of one pearl,"* seems to imply that this particular gate, which is probably every third or fourth one, is made out of one gigantic pearl.

Of course, in the natural, there is no such thing as a pearl that large; however, we limit God when we place Him in a category of inability. The Lord can do whatever He so desires. He is almighty. The fact is this: whatever it is that God has said He will do, to be certain, He shall do.

PURE GOLD

The phrase, *"And the street of the city was pure gold, as it were transparent glass,"* refers to the fact that not only are all the buildings of *"pure gold"* (Rev. 21:18), but, as well, even the streets are made of pure gold.

The gold that was applied to the tabernacle and the temple of old, whether in the furnishings or whatever, always symbolized the deity of Christ. With that being the case, with the entire New Jerusalem being pure gold, we are made to know more than ever exactly as to whom this *"Lion of the tribe of Judah,"* this *"Root of David"* actually is (Rev. 5:5).

The Scripture emphatically states that it is pure gold. The purity of the gold typifies the purity of the place and, therefore, the purity of Christ. As well, it typifies all who have trusted Him. In fact, it is so pure that it is like transparent glass.

Such is our salvation! It is a perfect salvation because it was instituted by the perfection of God and carried out by the perfect sacrifice of Christ on the Cross. As well, as the city is all of gold, salvation is all of God and none of man. While we are privileged to have it, it did not originate with us, in fact, because it could not originate with us. Pollution cannot bring forth purity. Perfection alone can bring forth purity, but it must be perfection that is poured out at the Cross, which it was in the form of the perfect, unstained blood of our Lord and Saviour, Jesus Christ.

As I journey through the land singing as I go,
Pointing souls to Calvary—to the crimson flow,
Many arrows pierce my soul from without, within;
But my Lord leads me on, through Him I must win.

When in service to my Lord dark may be the night,
But I'll cling more close to Him, He will give me light;
Satan's snares may vex my soul, turn my thoughts aside;
But my Lord goes ahead, leads whatever betide.

When in valleys low I look toward the mountain height,
And behold my Saviour there, leading in the fight,
With a tender hand outstretched toward the valley low,
Guiding me, I can see, as I onward go.

When before me billows rise from the mighty deep,
Then my Lord directs my bark; He does safely keep.
And He leads me gently on through this world below;
He's a real friend to me, Oh I love Him so.

Oh I want to see Him, look upon His face,
There to sing forever, of His saving grace;
On the streets of glory let me lift my voice,
Cares all past,
Home at last,
Ever to rejoice.

THE NEW JERUSALEM

CHAPTER 3

LORD GOD ALMIGHTY

LORD GOD ALMIGHTY

"AND I SAW NO temple therein: for the Lord God Almighty and the Lamb are the temple of it" (Rev. 21:22).

NO TEMPLE

The phrase, *"And I saw no temple therein,"* refers to a temple such as was in Old Testament times. Actually, there is a literal temple in the New Jerusalem (Rev. 3:12; 7:15; 11:19; 14:15, 17; 15:1-8; 16:1, 17). The meaning is that there is no temple there serving the same purpose as the temple served in the earthly Jerusalem, or even the millennial Jerusalem. Such is no longer necessary. The next phrase tells us why.

THE LORD GOD ALMIGHTY AND THE LAMB

The phrase, *"For the Lord God Almighty and the Lamb are the temple of it,"* presents the fact that the purpose of the temple that was erected on earth in Jerusalem in Old Testament times was for the purpose of worshipping God. At that time, God dwelt in the Holy of Holies between the mercy seat and the cherubim. Due to the fact that the sin debt had not yet been paid, and because the blood of bulls and goats could not take away sins, man, who was sinful, could not come into the direct presence of God lest he die. In other words, sinful man could not come into the presence of a thrice-holy God. So, a temple was needed in order for God to communicate with man, which He did through the ministry of the high priest.

In other words, the high priest in Israel of old was meant to be a type of Christ, who served as a mediator between God and men. However, when Christ came and died on the Cross, which took away all sin (Jn. 1:29), then the temple and the high priest (or any priest for that matter) were no longer needed. All of this was meant to typify Christ and His coming and the sacrifice of Himself on the Cross. This made unnecessary all the rudiments of old, which were meant only to be temporary anyway.

AFTER THE CROSS

After the Cross, with the sin debt being paid, upon faith in Christ, the individual is born again. This means that he is justified by faith, which makes it possible for the Holy Spirit to come into the believer on a permanent basis and dwell there (Jn. 14:16).

During the coming kingdom age when Christ will personally rule from Jerusalem, and will do so for 1,000 years, the temple will be rebuilt and the sacrifices reinstituted. However, all of this will be symbolic, meant to point to what Christ is in reality. Unfortunately, during the millennial reign, there will still be sin on the earth because there will be hundreds of millions of people who will actually not accept Christ as their Lord and Saviour. These people will not be allowed to destroy the peace of that particular time, but they will not be forced to give their hearts to the Lord as such. In fact, they cannot be forced. Incidentally, the kingdom age and millennial reign are two terms for the same event.

THE KINGDOM AGE

As Ezekiel portrays in the last nine chapters of his book, the entirety of the time frame of the millennial reign will be for the expressed purpose of portraying Christ as King. He will occupy the throne of David exactly as it was predicted (II Sam., Chpt. 7). He will, as well, at that time serve as prophet and high priest.

Also, there will be no great Day of Atonement in millennial worship, for the sacrifices then will recall the one all-sufficing atonement perfected at Golgotha.

As the Levitical offerings predicted the preciousness and sufficiency of the offering of Christ Himself, so will the millennial sacrifices recall and testify to that great offering as an accomplished fact.

These sacrifices will be necessary, for when Israel and the nations look upon the resplendent form of Immanuel at that time as He will appear on this mount of glory, they will be disposed to forget that He hung in blood and death for their sins upon the Cross of Calvary. We continue to talk about the millennial reign and the earthly Jerusalem of that day.

This great blood-sprinkled altar (Ezek. 43:18), with its burning fire, will vividly serve as a reminder to the entirety of the world. It will help them to feel that they are sinners, and we speak of the unredeemed, and that the precious blood of the Lamb of God shed for them is the one and only and necessary atonement and the foundation of all their millennial happiness.

ISRAEL

Israel restored in the coming millennial reign will be the premiere nation in the world of that day. It will be the priestly nation, pointing the entirety of the world to Christ.

Further, the reason for the necessity of the temple at that time and the instituting of the sacrifices once again may be a divine necessity. Israel, having in the past failed to observe the legislation of Leviticus and so to testify of the one great sacrifice that was to come, namely Christ, must by the perfect observance of the future sacrifices witness of an atoning Saviour, who has come. Thus, Calvary will be shown to be the divine center of God's purposes of grace and wrath. It is conceivable that only by such object lessons will it be possible to interpret the book of Leviticus to the various nations of the millennial earth and in this way, to vindicate God's action in the past and in the future.

THE NEW JERUSALEM

However, now that we come to the perfect age where

there is no more sin or the possibility of sin, the Lord God Almighty can, as well, dwell with men. Due to that fact, there is no need for a temple, at least as it regards worship, and that is for all the obvious reasons. However, it should be made clear that all of this is made possible by what Jesus did at the Cross, hence, Him being referred to as the Lamb. As the great voice said, *"Behold, the tabernacle of God is with men, and He will dwell with them, and they shall be His people, and God Himself shall be with them, and be their God"* (Rev. 21:3).

In Revelation 21:9, the Lamb is redemption. In Verse 14, the Lamb is the foundation. In Verse 22, the Lamb is the temple.

THE SUN AND THE MOON

"And the city had no need of the sun, neither of the moon, to shine in it: for the glory of God did lighten it, and the Lamb is the light thereof" (Rev. 21:23).

Verse 23 proclaims the fact that the Creator is not in need of His creation. God has need of nothing, but all have need of God.

It does not say in this passage that there will be no more sun or moon in the sky. It just simply refers to the fact that the light of such is not needed in the city. As an example, it will be like a coal oil lamp up beside an electric lightbulb. You could turn the coal oil lamp on or off, and it wouldn't make any difference either way simply because the electric bulb is so bright that it cancels out the other.

THE GLORY OF GOD AND THE LAMB

The phrase, *"For the glory of God did lighten it, and the Lamb is the light thereof,"* proclaims in fullness what there was only a glimmer of on the Mount of Transfiguration (Lk. 9:29).

Once again, John used the word *Lamb,* signifying that all of this is made possible for believers as a result of what Christ did at the Cross. In other words, we will enjoy the glory of God and the light of the Lamb forever and forever because of the Cross.

All of this of which we speak has always existed, for this is the abode of God; however, there is no way it could be made possible to human beings other than by what Christ did at the Cross and our acceptance of Him as our Lord and Saviour.

As well, we must remember that Christ is all of these things, as glorious as they are, as the Man, Christ Jesus (Rev. 5:5). And yet, at the same time, He is God; however, He will function forever as a man, although never ceasing to be God.

NATIONS

"And the nations of them which are saved shall walk in the light of it: and the kings of the earth do bring their glory and honor into it" (Rev. 21:24).

The phrase, *"And the nations of them which are saved shall walk in the light of it,"* should have been translated, *"And the nations shall walk by means of its light."* The words *"of them which are saved"* are not actually in the best manuscripts. In fact, there will be no one in the world of that day who isn't saved.

There is indication from this passage and a number of others that there will be natural people on the earth at that time who will carry out the original program of God as Adam and others would have done if man had not sinned.

With that being the case, there will actually be four classes of beings in the new heavens and the new earth. They are:

1. Deity, which is God the Father, God the Son, and God the Holy Spirit.
2. Angels, as well as the cherubim and seraphim.
3. The glorified saints of God, which will consist of every child of God who had part in the first resurrection. This will include all the redeemed from the time of Abel to the last person saved in the great tribulation.
4. There will be what we refer to as "natural people" who will be exactly as individuals today, except these individuals will be those who gave their hearts to Christ during the millennial reign. This will include most all Jews, as well as many Gentiles. Having accepted the Lord Jesus Christ as their personal Saviour, they will be given eternal life. They will live in this natural, eternal state forever. They will bear children who also will never die, who, in effect, will be sons and daughters of God.

There will not be any sin, temptation, wickedness, or evil of any nature in this perfect age to come, and, in fact, it will remain this way forever and forever.

THE KINGS OF THE EARTH

The phrase, *"And the kings of the earth do bring their glory and honor into it,"* refers to leaders of nations, whatever they might be called at that particular time. All will give glory to God, and all will honor the Lord, and do so forever.

THE GATES

"And the gates of it shall not be shut at all by day: for there shall be no night there" (Rev. 21:25).

The phrase, *"And the gates of it shall not be shut at all by day,"* gives a hint of the activity of commerce 24 hours a day. Now, exactly what that means as it regards the perfect age to come, considering the economy of the New Jerusalem, it would be impossible to presently comprehend such commerce. The fact of the entirety of this city being pure gold completely changes the idea of currency as we presently understand such. Also, that there is no war, sickness, death, or dying places a different complexion over everything. As well, transportation at that time, at least as it regards the glorified saints, will be at the speed of thought. In other words, if one wants to be someplace else, one merely thinks it, and one is there.

Of course, with there being no sin or Satan whatsoever, there will be, as well, no curse at all on the earth, which means that its productivity will be beyond compare.

As I attempt in the feebleness of our present position to explain this that John gave to us, I am overwhelmed. I greatly sense the presence of God even as I study these passages. I would pray that it would affect you in the same manner.

The dream of man will finally be realized, but it's all brought about by what Christ did at the Cross. This we must never forget!

NIGHT

The phrase, *"For there shall be no night there,"* pertains to the city itself, but with day and night continuing over the balance of the earth forever (Gen. 1:14-18; 8:22).

How can there be night there when the glory of God and of the Lamb shines perpetually? There's an old song that says:

> *There's a country far beyond the starry sky,*
> *There's a city where there never comes a night;*
> *If we're faithful we shall go there by and by,*
> *In the city where the Lamb is the light.*

GLORY AND HONOR

"And they shall bring the glory and honor of the nations into it" (Rev. 21:26).

The phrase, *"And they shall bring the glory and honor,"* refers to all things that are good. In fact, there will be nothing in that city, or even in the world of that day, that will hurt, harm, or cause problems and difficulties in any fashion.

The glory and honor of mankind presently are mostly

only contrived. There is too much sin and shame for it to be otherwise. In fact, other than that which is truly of the Lord, there is really no such thing as any actual glory and honor as it regards this present world. To be sure, what man refers to as glory and honor, as should be obvious, is not referred to by God in that fashion.

THE NATIONS

The phrase, *"Of the nations into it,"* proclaims a righteous commerce in every fashion.

The idea is that the New Jerusalem and, in fact, the perfect earth, which constitutes a perfect age, will remain this way forever and forever. There will never again be anything that will enter into it that defiles, is an abomination, or that which is a lie. Such evil will be forever gone.

Only they which are written in the Lamb's Book of Life will occupy this city, the world, and the perfect age. We have the promise of God here that *"It is done"* (Rev. 21:6).

PERFECTION

"And there shall in no wise enter into it anything that defiles, neither whatsoever works abomination, or makes a lie: but they which are written in the Lamb's book of life" (Rev. 21:27).

Verse 27 does not mean to insinuate, as some have claimed, that outside of the city such sin and iniquity exists.

In fact, there is absolutely nothing in the New Jerusalem or the entirety of the earth at that time that falls into this category.

The idea as presented here is that what caused the terrible fall to begin with, and we speak of the garden of Eden, will never happen again. God has given His word and promise that defilement, abominations, and all lies are a thing of the past and will never again have access to the present.

THE LAMB'S BOOK OF LIFE

The phrase, *"But they which are written in the Lamb's book of life,"* refers to the book of the redeemed. The word *Lamb* refers to the fact that all are saved by placing their faith and trust in Christ and what Christ did for us at the Cross. This is the criterion for entrance into that book, and all whose names are written in that book have eternal life, all afforded by the Lord Jesus Christ.

This plainly tells us that there will be no one in that world to come who is not born again and, thereby, perfectly righteous, and made so by the blood of the Lamb. As well, it's going to remain that way.

THE WATER OF LIFE

"And he showed me a pure river of water of life, clear as crystal, proceeding out of the throne of God and of the Lamb" (Rev. 22:1).

The phrase, *"And he showed me a pure river of water of*

life, clear as crystal," proclaims the fact that this river begins at the throne of God, which is, no doubt, at the pinnacle of this city. That means that it is some 1,500 miles high. Quite probably, this river, beginning at the throne, winds its way around this mountain, even winding again and again as it gradually drops the 1,500 miles. It probably branches off into 12 streams, which stop at each gate, or maybe they continue throughout the entirety of the earth, which is probably what will happen. As is obvious, we are given no particulars, so the best we can do is surmise.

Inasmuch as the Holy Spirit through John identified this river as water of life, we must come to the conclusion that it has life-giving properties. In fact, that is almost certain to be the case.

As we've already alluded, there will be millions of people in the new earth who will not have glorified bodies, and there will be untold billions who will be born throughout the ceaseless ages who, as well, will not have glorified bodies. However, they do have eternal life, as all will at that time, which will be sustained by the drinking of this water of life.

So, this means that this will be literal water, but yet, totally unlike any water that anyone has ever known or seen.

In fact, salvation, even in the spiritual sense, is referred to as *"living water."*

Jesus said: *"If any man thirst, let him come unto Me, and drink. He who believes on Me, as the Scripture has said, out of his belly* (innermost being) *shall flow rivers of living water"* (Jn. 7:37-38).

John then said, *"But this spoke He of the Spirit, which they who believe on Him should receive"* (Jn. 7:39).

So, this river will be a type of the Holy Spirit.

THE THRONE OF GOD AND OF THE LAMB

The phrase, *"proceeding out of the throne of God and of the Lamb,"* tells us by the use of the word *Lamb* that this river of the water of life is made possible, at least as it regards its life-giving properties given to individuals, by what Jesus did at the Cross.

One can, no doubt, say without fear of contradiction that all of these glorious things that pertain to God have always existed; however, what Jesus did at the Cross made it possible for mankind to enjoy all of these great blessings. This city has always been in heaven, but before the Cross, no human being could be brought to this glorious place. However, Jesus died on the Cross, thereby, settling the sin debt once and for all, at least for all who will believe. From the moment Christ died on the Cross, when the believer dies, his soul and spirit instantly go to be with the Lord in this glorious city. Of course, when the rapture takes place, all the redeemed will be transported to that particular place.

However, during the time we are discussing, this great city has come down to a new earth. In this renovated heaven and earth, all things are here exactly as they are in heaven. So, God can now change His headquarters from heaven to earth, which He will do at an appointed time.

THE TRINITY

Incidentally, in Verse 1 of Chapter 22, we have a clear presentation of the Trinity. It was the Holy Spirit who inspired John to write these words, and, as well, we have a portrayal of the throne of God where God the Father is and the Lamb—God the Son. However, there is just one throne, not two, etc. The one throne proclaims the fact of equality as it regards God the Father and God the Son. This means that their rule is equal.

IN THE MIDDLE OF THE STREET

"In the midst of the street of it, and on either side of the river, was there the Tree of Life, which bear twelve manner of fruits, and yielded her fruit every month: and the leaves of the tree were for the healing of the nations" (Rev. 22:2).

The phrase, *"In the midst of the street of it,"* proclaims the fact that this pure river of water of life, clear as crystal, flows in the middle of this street of pure gold. So, however the street goes from the throne of God, which it evidently does, down to the 12 gates below, the river flows accordingly.

If the street winds around the mountain, for it is a golden mountain, on its descent to the plain below, then the length could well be several thousands of miles.

This street is pure gold, and so pure, in fact, that it is transparent. Then, this pure river, as clear as crystal, flows in the middle of this street. When you consider the street of pure gold, the river as clear as crystal, and the trees, the beauty is absolutely indescribable!

How wide this river will be, we aren't told. We know that Ezekiel's river, which will flow from the temple in the millennial reign, is a little over one mile wide. Quite possibly this one will be at least that wide, or possibly even wider.

THE TREE OF LIFE

The phrase, *"And on either side of the river, was there the Tree of Life,"* corresponds with the water of life.

The idea is this: Along with drinking the water of life, and the Scripture doesn't say how often this should be, it seems that the fruit of the Tree of Life must be eaten every month as well. Of course, we're speaking of the part of the population that doesn't have glorified bodies.

FRUITS

The phrase, *"which bear twelve manner of fruits, and yielded her fruit every month,"* refers to a different fruit each month. There are 12 different types of fruit, but we aren't told what they are.

We have the number 12 again, which signifies the government of God as it relates to the manner of eternal life as it refers to the individuals in question.

THE LEAVES AND HEALING

The phrase, *"and the leaves of the tree were for the healing of the nations,"* pertains to the stopping of any type of sickness before it even begins, even as the water of life and the

Tree of Life pertain to youthfulness and, thereby, eternal life.

As it regards age of individuals in the perfect age to come, it is my personal belief that everyone will be 33 and a half years old, at least as we count years presently.

I derive that from the words of John: *"Beloved, now are we the sons of God, and it does not yet appear what we shall be: but we know that, when He shall appear, we shall be like Him; for we shall see Him as He is"* (I Jn. 3:2).

Jesus was 33 and a half years old (or approximately so) when He ascended to go back to heaven. John said that we will be like Him, and quite possibly, that pertains to age throughout the eternal ages as well.

LITTLE INFANTS

It should be obvious that little infants and the aged in years will not remain that way pertaining to this coming time. The infant will be brought to maturity, even as the aged will be brought to youthfulness. This goes for the glorified saints, as well as those we refer to as natural people.

I suppose I could say it in this manner: From the description given in these passages, it seems as though families with babies being born will continue forever and forever. With no sickness and death due to the water of life and the Tree of Life, along with the leaves, which are for healing, all will stop aging at 33 and a half years old.

We must remember that the glory of God shall permeate the New Jerusalem and, no doubt, the entire earth at that particular time. This within itself is of such magnitude as to defy description.

A DREAM

Without going into much detail, some years ago I had a dream of heaven.

A dear lady, a friend of ours, had died, and in the dream, we accompanied her to heaven. Frances was with me, along with Frances' mother.

I recollect that in the dream, I was explaining to our friend what the Lord had prepared for her in that eternal abode. I then told her that we had to go back to our lives on earth, but we would be back at a particular time.

The thing I remember so vividly about the dream is the following: The very air was permeated with the glory of God. It was the most restful, relaxing, secure, and glorious feeling of well-being that I have ever experienced. It was so beautiful and so wonderful that I didn't want to leave. It was as though I was perfectly at home, and that feeling I will never forget. It was the glory of God, and perpetual glory at that.

Even now in prayer, oftentimes, I will sense the same identical feeling and spirit that I sensed in that dream those years ago. Many times, I will go to prayer with problems and difficulties weighing heavily upon me. Almost all of these things require the help of the Lord, and miraculous help at that. However, oftentimes, in a few minutes, the presence of God, which, of course, is the glory of God, will begin to fill my soul.

The same feeling of security and well-being will come over me as it did in that dream. Most of the time, it will last for hours.

Whatever the problems are, it's as if they recede into the background, if remaining at all! However, the thing I wish to impress upon you the reader is that the glory of God, which we are privileged to experience at this particular time in a limited manner, will then be perpetual and eternal.

NO MORE CURSE

"And there shall be no more curse: but the throne of God and of the Lamb shall be in it; and His servants shall serve Him" (Rev. 22:3).

The phrase, *"And there shall be no more curse,"* refers back to Adam's sin when God said, *"Cursed is the ground for your sake"* (Gen. 3:17).

In fact, the curse will be lifted in the coming kingdom age, which is the age that immediately precedes the perfect age. Concerning the kingdom age, the prophet Isaiah said, *"Instead of the thorn shall come up the fir tree, and instead of the brier shall come up the myrtle tree"* (Isa. 55:13).

The idea of the statement given in Verse 3, *"And there shall be no more curse,"* simply states the fact that never again will there be a curse, as never again will there be *"anything that defiles, neither whatsoever works abomination, or makes a lie"* (Rev. 21:27).

Even with the curse presently on the earth, and it definitely continues to exist, we are told that it is possible for this present

earth to feed 100 billion people. So, even now, there is no reason for anyone to go hungry; however, due to the fact that
many, if not most, of the nations of the world are governed
by demon spirits, which can do nothing but steal, kill, and
destroy, productivity is greatly hindered, as would be obvious.

When we consider that in the perfect age to come there
will be no more curse, then we can see that the potential for
productivity at that coming time will be so absolutely phe-
nomenal as to defy all description. No more curse means that
the entirety of the earth will become a fertile field without des-
erts. We might quickly add that there will be no more thorns
and thistles or anything of that nature. As well, we must consider that the landmass will be increased severalfold due to
the fact that there will be no more great oceans. So, the man
speaking to John matter-of-factly says, *"And there shall be no
more curse,"* guaranteeing that such belongs to the past and
will never again be present in the future.

THE THRONE OF GOD AND OF THE LAMB

The phrase, *"but the throne of God and of the Lamb shall
be in it,"* presents, as previously stated, one throne and not
two. The idea of this is, even as we have already stated, the
authority of rulership will be as great with God the Son as it is
with God the Father.

Also, the curse being lifted is all because of what Jesus
did at Calvary. In fact, what Christ did there is constituted as
a covenant, which means that it goes into perpetuity. That's

why Paul labeled it as the everlasting covenant (Heb. 13:20). In fact, the apostle referred to this as *"the blood of the everlasting covenant."*

As the Lamb has made possible the water of life of Verse 1, the Lamb in this verse guarantees that *"there shall be no more curse."*

SERVANTS

The phrase, *"And His servants shall serve Him,"* goes back to Exodus, Chapter 21.

This speaks of servants in a Hebrew household. Some who were set free loved their masters to such an extent, and appreciated their place and position to such an extent, that instead of leaving, they desired to stay.

In that case, the servant desiring such was to be brought *"to the door, or unto the doorpost; and his master shall bore his ear through with an aul; and he shall serve him forever"* (Ex. 21:5-6).

As is obvious, this is a voluntary servanthood.

So, the idea is that every believer in the perfect age will so love the Lord and the Lamb that all will gladly serve Him. The idea should be very obvious: This greatness, this grandness, and this glory that every believer will have, and will have forever, were made possible by what Jesus did at the Cross. Without His great sacrifice of Himself, every last mother's son and every last father's daughter would have been eternally lost. We owe everything to Christ!

It is beautiful that the last time the word *Lamb* is used, it is used in the sense of what Christ did at the Cross, which forever removed the curse, and how that every believer will gladly serve Him forever.

TO SEE HIS FACE

"And they shall see His face; and His name shall be in their foreheads" (Rev. 22:4).

The phrase, *"And they shall see His face,"* refers to relationship totally unlike that of what we normally think as it regards servants. This refers to the fact that Christ will be available to all, and that all in a sense hold the same standing and status. It has to be this way simply because all are in Christ!

The first inhabitants of earth hid themselves from the face of God. Its future occupants shall see the face of God, and it's all because of what Jesus did at the Cross. To be able to look God in the face speaks of justification by faith. It speaks of a total and complete exoneration, meaning that the person is no longer guilty, and he can, therefore, look straight into the eyes of God.

FOREHEADS

The phrase, *"And His name shall be in their foreheads,"* refers to ownership. The 144,000 are also said to have the *"Father's name written in their foreheads"* (Rev. 14:1). And so, in effect, all believers will function accordingly.

Will this be literal?

I doubt that it speaks of being literal. I think it speaks more of ownership. The Lord owns us, and because He paid such a price for our redemption, in one sense of the word, we also own Him. Jesus said, *"At that day you shall know that I am in My Father, and you in Me, and I in you"* (Jn. 14:20).

NO NIGHT

"And there shall be no night there; and they need no candle, neither light of the sun; for the Lord God gives them light: and they shall reign forever and ever" (Rev. 22:5).

The phrase, *"And there shall be no night there,"* proclaims the third time this is stated or implied (Rev. 21:23, 25). The repetition is not without meaning.

The emphasis is not so much on the fact that there is no night there, but rather what causes such to be brought about. The cause is the glory of God and the Lamb. In fact, the Scripture emphatically states, *"And the Lamb is the light thereof"* (Rev. 21:23).

Jesus Christ is the Creator of all things (Jn. 1:1-3), but added to His role as Creator is the role of Saviour, which was brought about by what He did at the Cross (Jn. 1:29).

One cannot better perfection, and Christ has always been perfect. However, things can be added to perfection, and this is exactly what happened to Christ.

As Creator, He was perfect in all things, but He has had the role of Saviour added to His position as Creator.

Consequently, in the role of the latter, for this is what the word *Lamb* actually means: He is the light. In fact, the status of the New Jerusalem hasn't really changed. It has always been this way; however, what He did at the Cross made it possible for believers to enjoy this light, i.e., the presence of God.

NO OTHER LIGHT NEEDED

The phrase, *"And they need no candle, neither light of the sun; for the Lord God gives them light,"* presents the source of this light. To be sure, the sun will continue to shine, but the light furnished by the Lord will be of such great illumination that at night, it will be just as bright as the day. As previously stated, it seems that this will be in the New Jerusalem only, with the balance of the earth continuing to function as God originally created. Concerning this, the Bible says:

> *And God said, Let there be lights in the firmament of the heaven to divide the day from the night; and let them be for signs, and for seasons, and for days, and years: And let them be for lights in the firmament of the heaven to give light upon the earth: and it was so. And God made two great lights; the greater light to rule the day, and the lesser light to rule the night: He made the stars also. And God set them in the firmament of the heaven to give light upon the earth, and to rule over the day and over the night, and to divide the light from the darkness: and God saw that it was good (Gen. 1:14-18).*

There is no record in the Word of God that God has changed this order or will change this order. In the city itself, yes, He will, but in the balance of the earth, no, He will not.

REIGN

The phrase, *"And they shall reign forever and ever,"* refers to the servants of Revelation 22:3.

Some have contended that the servants of Verse 3 are angels; however, the personal pronouns of Verses 4 and 5 proclaim the fact that the servants rather are believers. It has never been known for servants to reign like kings, etc., but these servants shall!

So, even though we are slaves of Jesus Christ, for that's what the word *servant* means here, we are at the same time children of God: *"And if children, then heirs; heirs of God, and joint-heirs with Christ; if so be that we suffer with Him, that we may be also glorified together"* (Rom. 8:17).

By adoption, we are children—children of God. By choice, we are servants.

FAITHFUL AND TRUE

"And he said unto me, These sayings are faithful and true: and the Lord God of the holy prophets sent His angel to show unto His servants the things which must shortly be done" (Rev. 22:6).

The word *angel* should have been translated *messenger* (this is proven by Revelation 22:9). And, as we see in Verse 8 of the same chapter, John fell down to worship him, thinking perhaps he was Christ. He was forbidden to do so.

The phrase, *"And he said unto me, These sayings are faithful and true,"* is proclaimed in this fashion simply because many of the statements made are so absolutely astounding that they defy description. However, despite the statements being incredulous, they are faithful and true. In other words, all written here will come to pass exactly as stated.

One of the names of Christ is *"Faithful and True"* (Rev. 19:11), which means that He guarantees the veracity of these descriptions.

MUST SHORTLY BE DONE

The phrase, *"And the Lord God of the holy prophets sent His angel to show unto His servants the things which must shortly be done,"* is not translated properly.

The Greek word *aggelos,* translated *angel,* should have been translated *messenger.* Again, we know from what he says in Verse 9 that this man was not an angel, and neither was he Christ.

The phrase, *"which must shortly be done,"* presents itself as confusing to some. He was not speaking of John's day and forward, which now would total approximately 1,900 years. He was speaking of the setting of the vision, the time frame of which has not come about even yet. In fact, this time frame that is the setting of this vision, and we speak of the entirety of the book of Revelation, takes place immediately after the rapture of the church. From that point forward, which is what is meant here, we have *"the things which must shortly be done,"* which refers to the great tribulation.

THE SECOND COMING

"Behold, I come quickly: blessed is he who keeps the sayings of the prophecy of this book" (Rev. 22:7).

The phrase, *"Behold, I come quickly,"* must be understood according to the time frame of which it speaks. Evidently, the man speaking to John was quoting what he knew to be the truth, possibly what He had personally heard the Master Himself say.

The phrase, *"Behold, I come quickly,"* has more to do with the manner of His coming than anything else. When He does come, which will be at the height of the battle of Armageddon, it will be sudden, even immediate.

THE PROPHECY OF THIS BOOK

The phrase, *"Blessed is he who keeps the sayings of the prophecy of this book,"* lets us know how important these predictions are. In fact, this is the only book in the world that gives a preview of the future; consequently, every believer ought to study the book of Revelation as much as they do any other book in the entirety of the Bible. We are promised a blessing at the beginning of this book if we do so (Rev. 1:3), and now the book closes with the same promise.

Someday the silver cord will break,
And I no more as now shall sing;
But Oh! The joy when I shall wake
Within the palace of the King!

Someday my earthly house will fall,
I cannot tell how soon 'twill be,
But this I know, my All-in-all
Has now a place in heaven for me.

Someday when fades the golden sun,
Beneath the rosy tinted west,
My blessed Lord will say, "Well done!"
And I shall enter into rest.

Some day: till then I'll watch and wait,
My lamp all trimmed and burning bright,
That when my Saviour opens the gate,
My soul to Him may take its flight.

THE NEW JERUSALEM

CHAPTER 4
ALPHA AND OMEGA

ALPHA AND OMEGA

"AND I JOHN SAW these things, and heard them. And when I had heard and seen, I fell down to worship before the feet of the angel which showed me these things" (Rev. 22:8).

EYEWITNESS

The phrase, *"And I John saw these things, and heard them,"* presents an impeccable witness. There is no more credible witness, that is, if that person is honest, than one who was at the scene of the situation and personally saw and heard. John saw many things, and he heard many things!

In other words, he was, in essence, saying that he had done his very best to give a proper account of what he saw and heard. He had not embellished it in any way, and neither had he limited in any way what he had been shown. He was saying that his testimony would stand up in any court of the land.

WORSHIP

The phrase, *"And when I had heard and seen, I fell down to worship before the feet of the angel which showed me these things,"* presents the apostle doing the same thing as he did in Revelation 19:10, but as we shall see, the man here is different than the one in the previous verse.

Why would John make the same mistake twice?

I personally think that John was so overawed by what he had seen and heard, as would be any individual, that he had difficulty putting everything in proper perspective.

When these visions began to come, the first appearance was of Christ. John explained what he saw and then said: *"And when I saw Him, I fell at His feet as dead. And He laid His right hand upon me, saying unto me, Fear not; I am the first and the last"* (Rev. 1:17).

With the first appearance being of Christ and the other appearances by men who evidently looked very similar to Christ, it is my thought that the apostle hardly knew what to do. Due to the glory and grandeur of it all, he tried to worship two individuals who were actually human beings. Neither would allow him to continue.

WORSHIP GOD

"Then says he unto me, See you do it not: for I am your fellowservant, and of your brethren the prophets, and of them which keep the sayings of this book: worship God" (Rev. 22:9).

The phrase, *"Then says he unto me, See you do it not,"* presents the same words used by the previous man when John had done the same thing (Rev. 19:10). The man would not accept worship, and rightly so!

I have made allowances for the great apostle; however, George Williams, in his *Student's Commentary*, presents a different take on this situation. He says: "The incurable enslavement of the human heart to idolatry notwithstanding, here again appears (Rev. 19:10; 22:8). If the wisest monarch (Solomon) who ever lived, and who also was an inspired prophet, and if the most beloved of the apostles were by nature idolaters, how needful is it for all Christian people to watch against the smallest beginnings of this evil."

Possibly our brother is right, but concerning John the Beloved, I would certainly like to believe that he isn't. But yet, probably one can say that idolatry is the greatest religious sin there is.

IDOLATRY

Idolatry thrives where it is least expected. For instance, untold millions make idols out of their churches, denominations, particular preachers, etc. And then, pet sins become idols to individual Christians.

I personally believe that if the believer doesn't have a proper view of the Cross, it's virtually impossible to escape idolatry. Such a view places the individual in a proper perspective and, as well, gives Christ His proper place. A proper view of oneself and a proper view of Christ cannot be without the believer knowing and understanding the rudiments of the Cross. Unfortunately, such knowledge, at least at the present time, is almost nonexistent.

Of course, John knew and understood the Cross, actually having learned it from the Epistles of Paul. That's the reason I say that the apostle was confused as it regarded him attempting to worship the particular man in question. Then again, it is quite possible that the man looked so much like Christ, so much like an angel, etc., that it would have fooled basically anyone. Whatever the case, I don't think any idolatry was in the heart of John.

A PROPHET

The phrase, *"For I am your fellowservant, and of your brethren the prophets, and of them which keep the sayings of this book,"* presents this man as different from the one of Revelation 19:10. That one said, *"I am your fellowservant, and of your brethren."*

The former one adds the words, *"the prophets,"* referring to the fact that he evidently was one of the great prophets of the Old Testament. It could have been Isaiah, Jeremiah, Ezekiel, or even Daniel, and there were others as well!

All of this tells us several things:

- Due to the fact that these brethren who spoke with John had such vast knowledge, we are led to understand that our education is greatly enhanced after reaching heaven.

- This also tells us that there is no such thing as "soul sleep" taught in the Bible. The moment the believer dies, his soul and spirit instantly go to be with the Lord Jesus (Phil. 1:23).

- We learn from all of this that tremendous responsibility is accorded those who have gone on to be with the Lord. I might quickly add that these men who spoke with John, whomever they might have been, are still in heaven, and we will meet them when the trump sounds, for they, too, will be a part of the first resurrection. Then John will also know their identity.

By the man using the term, *"And of them which keep the sayings of this book,"* it tells us that he also eagerly awaits the fulfillment of these prophecies.

WORSHIP

The phrase, *"worship God,"* means that God alone must be worshipped. Of course, that would include both God the Father and God the Son. They alone are worthy of worship.

Because of what Jesus did at the Cross, the Holy Spirit, without fail, always directs worship to the Lord Jesus Christ, despite the fact that the Holy Spirit is also God. The reason for that is the price that was paid at Calvary's Cross. So, the record is that the Holy Spirit will not accept worship but will direct all to the Son of God, and for the reasons mentioned.

SEAL NOT

"And he said unto me, Seal not the sayings of the prophecy of this book: for the time is at hand" (Rev. 22:10).

The phrase, *"And he said unto me, Seal not the sayings of the prophecy of this book,"* refers to the fact that the things given in this book are meant to be known and understood. They are not hidden truths. They are simple and clear to all who will believe them, but they are hidden from those who refuse to believe (II Cor. 4:4).

IT IS TIME

The phrase, *"For the time is at hand,"* speaks of the immediate fulfillment of events that were to happen in consecutive order from John's day into eternity. The statement is somewhat different than the statement of Verse 6:

- Chapters 2 and 3 present the church age. We are now living in the very closing days of that particular time. The rapture could take place at any moment.

- The great tribulation will follow the rapture as outlined in Chapters 6 through 19.

- We then have the events of the thousand-year reign with Christ, which is the millennium, and then the new earth forever, which is the perfect age. It is an age, incidentally, that will never end. This is found in Chapters 20 through 22 of the great book of Revelation.

Actually, the book of Revelation has been in fulfillment from the very moment it was written, and it continues to be fulfilled even as I write these words.

As previously stated, it is the only book in the world that gives detailed accounts of futuristic events as it regards the spirit world. It is meant to be mastered by the saints of God, for this is at least one of the reasons that the Lord gave the book.

UNJUST AND FILTHY

"He who is unjust, let him be unjust still: and he which is filthy, let him be filthy still: and he who is righteous, let him be righteous still: and he who is holy, let him be holy still" (Rev. 22:11).

The phrase, *"He who is unjust, let him be unjust still: and he which is filthy, let him be filthy still,"* proclaims the fact that men are building up their destinies by the actions and habits of their lives.

So, slowly but surely, the power of being masters of our fate passes out of our hands. It is in this law of our nature that the key to many of the darkest problems of the future may lie, but we must ever understand that the Word of God holds the answer and solution to all of these perplexing questions, whatever they might be.

The Bible plainly states that first, second, third, and fourth opportunities are on this side of the grave. There are no second chances after death. Consequently, there is no such thing as purgatory taught in the Bible. There is no such thing as people getting right with God after they are dead. If they are unjust when they die, they will continue to be unjust forever. If they are filthy, morally speaking, when they die, they will be filthy forever.

In Chapter 16 of Luke, Jesus told the story of the rich man and the beggar. The story is rather strange to us because we do not understand the Jewish culture of that day.

THE GREATEST ILLUSTRATION
OF LIFE AFTER DEATH

At that time, the Jews believed that if a fellow Jew was rich, that reflected the favor and blessing of God, and most certainly, he was saved. If he was a beggar such as Lazarus, that portrayed the curse of God, meaning the individual was lost. So, Jesus completely destroyed their doctrine by telling them that riches or poverty had nothing to do with one's salvation. In this case, the rich man was lost. He was not lost because he was rich. He was lost because he did not allow the goodness of God (his riches) to bring him to God. Even though Lazarus was a beggar and had received no creature comforts whatsoever in this life, he was saved. He did not allow his poverty to keep him from God.

Then Jesus finished the story by giving the chilling account of Lazarus being in paradise and the rich man being in hell. The prayer that the rich man prayed, *"Father Abraham, have mercy on me, and send Lazarus"* (Lk. 16:24), is the only example in Scripture of praying to a dead saint. Let those who do this remember that such a prayer will avail the same as it did then—nothing.

As the Word of God is closed with the last book of the Bible, the Holy Spirit is solemnly reminding us that if we are basing our hope on a second or third chance after death, it is a fool's hope. What we are before death is what we will be forever in eternity. If one is not washed in the blood of the Lamb at the time of death, one will never be washed by the blood of the Lamb.

THE CRY OF THE HOLY SPIRIT

In these closing comments, which serve as a typical direction of the entirety of the Bible, the Holy Spirit is telling the entirety of mankind that the unjust and morally filthy can be changed by the power of God. Man does not have to remain in this dilemma. Unjustness can be changed to righteousness, and moral filth can be changed to holiness. In fact, this is the very tenor of the gospel.

Jesus died on a cruel Cross, thereby, satisfying the demands of heavenly justice, which paid the debt of the broken law and, thereby, atoned for all sin. It was a fearful and frightful price that had to be paid for man to be saved. The two words—*unjust* and *filthy*—morally describe the human race. It is a result of the fall and is so deep-seated in man that it is his very nature—the sin nature. It cannot be changed or assuaged by the change of environment, education, or with money. In fact, man's nature of unjustness and moral filthiness is absolutely unchangeable as far as man is concerned. It can be changed only by God and only by man accepting Christ and what Christ has done for him at the Cross. Otherwise, he who is unjust, let him be unjust still, and he who is filthy, let him be filthy still!

RIGHTEOUS AND HOLY

The phrase, *"And he who is righteous, let him be righteous still: and he who is holy, let him be holy still,"* records that which the Spirit of God can bring about in a person's life, irrespective of the fact that they have once been unjust and morally filthy. As stated, only the power of God can bring about such a state.

Man within himself has no righteousness and, in fact, cannot attain to righteousness by any means, at least of his own machinations. A polluted spring cannot bring forth pure water.

So man cannot change his situation by his own personal efforts. It doesn't matter how many New Year's resolutions he makes or his trying to turn over a new leaf, so to speak. He is doomed to continue in the direction in which he is unless he turns to Christ. In other words, there is no such thing as moral evolution. Even though it's possibly the greatest topic in America and the world today, it is a wasted effort, no matter the procedure. Man cannot gradually get better by situations and systems that he may employ. Only God can better a person.

In fact, it is possible for an individual to be totally unrighteous one minute and completely righteous the next. It is all done by faith, and I speak of faith in Jesus Christ and Him crucified (Jn. 3:16; Rom. 5:1-2; Eph. 2:8-9).

RIGHTEOUSNESS

Upon turning to Christ, the miracle of transformation takes place. It is called the born-again experience (Jn. 3:3). At that time, a work of regeneration is carried out by the Holy

Spirit in one's life, which sanctifies that person. This refers to *making* one clean (morally clean). It, as well, justifies one, which *declares* him clean. This is all done by faith in the Cross of Christ (I Cor. 6:9-11).

This is the only way that a state of righteousness can be attained. Let the reader understand that because if any other way is proposed, it is a fool's way.

With righteousness comes a state of holiness, which refers to one being set apart exclusively for the Lord. This means that one is pulled away completely from unjustness and moral filthiness.

A state of holiness or sainthood is instantly given to the believing sinner upon confession of Christ. It is not something that one works toward but that which is freely imputed. It is all made possible by what Jesus did at the Cross and faith in that finished work!

Faith in Christ guarantees the standing of righteousness and holiness (Gal. 6:14). Faith in Christ alone attains righteousness and holiness, and faith in Christ alone maintains righteousness and holiness. Let us say it again: there is no such thing as moral evolution.

OBEDIENCE

Millions of Christians have it in their minds that such a state is achieved and maintained by obedience in the keeping of the commandments, etc. While, of course, obedience is exactly what must be, let the reader understand that within one's own capabilities, obedience is impossible. Now, let's say that again because it is so very, very important.

I don't care who the person is or how consecrated to the Lord he may conclude himself to be. Within his own strength and ability, there is no way he can properly be obedient to the Lord. It just simply cannot be done. To be sure, it can be done and, in fact, must be done, but only in one way.

Obedience to God, which is most definitely demanded, is gained only in Christ and what He has done for us at the Cross. What do we mean by that?

All that we need to do as it regards the keeping of the commandments and our daily living, which constitutes our walk before God, has already been done in Christ simply because it could only be done in Christ. He has fully, totally, completely, and absolutely kept all the commandments, and He has kept them perfectly. It was all done on our behalf. In other words, every single thing He did was done exclusively as our substitute. The truth is, we couldn't do it ourselves, so our representative man had to do it for us, and He, to be sure, did it perfectly (I Cor. 15:45-47).

Consequently, I am given His perfect obedience, for that's exactly what He rendered to God. The first Adam rendered disobedience, and the last Adam rendered a perfect obedience. As stated, it was done on our behalf, even as our substitute.

When I exhibit faith in what Christ did at the Cross, everything He has done is made available to me. To be sure, this is all made possible to me by what He did at the Cross. Actually, in the mind of God, when I expressed faith in Christ, I was literally baptized into His death. That doesn't speak of water baptism, but rather the crucifixion of Christ. This is the reason that His crucifixion is paramount in the salvation process.

I was also *"buried with Him,"* which means the old man, with all of what I used to be, is forever gone. I was then raised with Him in *"newness of life"* (Rom. 6:3-5).

THE CROSS

Now, let the reader understand that all of this is made possible in my life by what Jesus did at the Cross, and that exclusively, and my faith in that finished work.

Understanding that it was all carried out at the Cross, in other words, that the old Jimmy Swaggart died in that process, I am then to reckon myself to be dead indeed unto sin but alive unto God through Jesus Christ my Lord (Rom. 6:11).

FAITH

The passage I have just referenced represents our faith, but let the reader understand that it must ever be faith in the Cross of Christ. If it's not faith in the Cross, then it's faith that God will never recognize.

I am dead unto sin, which means I am dead unto the sin nature, simply because of what Jesus did at the Cross and my faith in that great sacrifice. That is the bedrock of salvation and sanctification.

Continuing to function according to my faith in the

finished work of Christ, I have the assurance of the Word of God that sin shall not have dominion over me (Rom. 6:14).

THE HOLY SPIRIT

With my faith anchored in the sacrifice of Christ, I am then guaranteed the help of the Holy Spirit, who guarantees me victory in every aspect of my living for the Lord (Rom. 8:1-2, 11).

There is a law of sin and death that plagues the human race, and it is so powerful that man in his own ability cannot climb out of this terrible bondage. In fact, even if a Christian approaches it in the wrong way, he, as well, will be overcome.

There is only one law that is greater than the law of sin and death, and that is *"the law of the Spirit of life in Christ Jesus"* (Rom. 8:2).

This refers exclusively to what Christ did at the Cross, which means that the Holy Spirit works within these boundaries and these boundaries alone. It only requires my faith in Christ and His finished work, which, of course, speaks of the Cross. Maintaining faith in that great sacrifice guarantees the continued help of the Holy Spirit and guaranteed victory. That is the key to righteousness and holiness: The Cross! The Cross! The Cross!

I COME QUICKLY

"And, behold, I come quickly; and My reward is with Me, to give every man according as his work shall be" (Rev. 22:12).

The phrase, *"And, behold, I come quickly,"* is not meant to portray the time of His coming, but rather that the suddenness of the apparition of the Great Judge will be without warning.

It can speak of two things—the rapture of the church or the second coming. At the rapture, every saint of God will go to meet the Lord in the air. At the second coming, all the saints of God who have ever lived from the very beginning will be with Him.

The idea is that when the Lord comes, it will be without warning. In other words, there will be no signs given as it regards the rapture of the church. It is something that will happen instantly.

Paul said, and I quote the text and notes directly from The Expositor's Study Bible:

> *But I would not have you to be ignorant, brethren, concerning them which are asleep* (refers to believers who have died), *that you sorrow not, even as others which have no hope.* (This concerns those who do not know the Lord who will have no part in the first resurrection of life and, therefore, no hope for heaven.)

> *For if we believe that Jesus died and rose again* (the very foundation of Christianity is the death and resurrection of Christ; it is the proof of life after death in a glorified state for all saints in that life, which, incidentally, will never end), *even so them also which sleep in Jesus will God bring with Him.* (This refers to the rapture of the church, or

the resurrection of all believers, with both phrases meaning the same thing, even as Paul describes in I Corinthians,
Chapter 15. At death, the soul and the spirit of the child of
God instantly go to be with Jesus [Phil. 1:23], while the
physical body goes back to dust. At the rapture, God will
replace what was the physical body with a glorified body,
united with the soul and the spirit. In fact, the soul and the
spirit of each individual will accompany the Lord down
close to this earth to be united with a glorified body, which
will then make the believer whole.)

THE WORD OF THE LORD

For this we say unto you by the word of the Lord (presents the doctrine of the rapture of the church as the 'word
of the Lord'), *that we which are alive and remain unto
the coming of the Lord* (all believers who are alive at the
rapture) *shall not prevent them which are asleep.* (This
refers to the fact that the living saints will not precede or
go before the dead saints.)

*For the Lord Himself shall descend from heaven with
a shout* (refers to 'the same Jesus' which the angels proclaimed in Acts 1:11), *with the voice of the archangel*
(refers to Michael, the only one referred to as such [Jude,
vs. 9]), *and with the trump of God* (doesn't exactly say
God will personally blow this trumpet, but that it definitely does belong to Him, whoever does signal the

blast): *and the dead in Christ shall rise first* (the criteria for being ready for the rapture is to be 'in Christ,' which means that all who are truly born again will definitely go in the rapture):

Then we which are alive and remain shall be caught up (raptured) *together with them* (the resurrected dead) *in the clouds* (clouds of saints, not clouds as we normally think of such), *to meet the Lord in the air* (the Greek word for 'air' is 'aer' and refers to the lower atmosphere, or from about 6,000 feet down; so, the Lord will come at least within 6,000 feet of the earth as it regards the rapture, perhaps even lower, with all the saints meeting Him there; but He, at that time, will not come all the way to the earth, that awaiting the second coming, which will be seven or more years later): *and so shall we ever be with the Lord.* (This presents the greatest meeting humanity will have ever known.)

Wherefore comfort one another with these words. (This pertains to the future of the child of God, which is glorious indeed!) (I Thess. 4:13-18).

THE SECOND COMING

Once again I quote from The Expositor's Study Bible:

And I saw heaven opened (records the final prophetic hour regarding the second coming, without a doubt the greatest moment in human history), *and behold a white horse* (in effect, proclaims a warhorse [Zech. 14:3]); *and He who sat upon him was called Faithful and True* (faithful to His promises and true to His judgments; He contrasts with the false messiah of Revelation 6:2, who was neither faithful nor true), *and in righteousness He does judge and make war* (refers to the manner of His second coming).

His eyes were as a flame of fire (represents judgment), *and on His head were many crowns* (represents the fact that He will not be Lord of just one realm; He will be Lord of all realms); *and He had a name written, that no man knew, but He Himself* (not meaning that it is unknown, but rather it is definitely unknowable; it will remain unreachable to man, meaning that its depths can never be fully plumbed).

And He was clothed with a vesture dipped in blood (speaks of the Cross where He shed His life's blood, which gives Him the right to judge the world): *and His name is called the Word of God.* (His revealed name is the Word of God, for He revealed God in His grace and power to make Him known, so the believer can say, 'I know Him.')

And the armies which were in heaven followed Him upon white horses (these 'armies' are the saints of God, in fact, all the saints who have ever lived, meaning we will be with Him at the second coming), *clothed in fine linen, white and clean* (Rev. 19:11-14).

Incidentally, the second coming will take place during the battle of Armageddon, which will defeat the Antichrist. Christ will then set up a kingdom that will rule the world for a thousand years and then forever. He will rule from Jerusalem and will restore Israel to her rightful place, position, and power as the leading nation in the world.

REWARD

The phrase, *"And My reward is with Me,"* refers to the fact that it is the Lord who does the doing. As well, the word *reward* can either be positive or negative. Every man will be rewarded according to his conduct, and the eternal destiny of each will be fixed either as holiness or vileness. This is the spirit of the text. Jesus Christ is either Saviour or Judge! It is all in Him.

If men do not deal with Christ now as Saviour, they will deal with Him tomorrow as Judge, but deal with Him they shall! One way or the other, all will deal with Him.

WORKS

The phrase, *"To give every man according as his work shall be,"* tells us emphatically that our lifestyles will definitely produce a certain type of works.

Let the following be clearly understood: Good works will never produce proper faith, but proper faith will always produce proper works. Now, that is one of the most important statements that you as a believer will ever read.

Let's explain it further: Most of the church world attempts to produce righteousness (that is addressed in Verse 11) by works. That cannot be done! In fact, it is impossible for it to be done in this manner. What do I mean when I say that the church world attempts to produce righteousness and holiness by works?

I mean that we do religious things, and we think that by the doing of those things, such will make us righteous and holy. That means that we have faith in those things, whatever they might be.

Now, more than likely, the things of which we speak aren't wrong, but rather right. In other words, they are good things.

Please notice what Paul said: *"Was then that which is good made death unto me? God forbid. But sin, that it might appear sin, working death in me by that which is good"* (Rom. 7:13).

WHAT WAS PAUL TALKING ABOUT?

In this case, he's speaking of the Ten Commandments as given in the law of Moses (Rom. 7:10-12).

Now, many Christians may read that statement and automatically dismiss it because they would say that the law of Moses has nothing to do with us today, etc. In a sense, that's right, but in another sense, it's wrong.

Paul was writing here more so to Gentiles than to Jews. So, if what he was saying was apropos for Gentiles then, and it definitely was, then it's necessary for us presently.

The apostle asked the question: *"Was then that which is good* (he is continuing to speak of the commandments) *made death unto me?"* His answer was instant, *"God forbid!"* In other words, he was saying that the commandments of God aren't sinful, wicked, or wrong.

So, I'll say the following: The good things that we do, such as faithfulness to church, reading so many chapters each day in the Bible, paying our tithes, witnessing to souls, or setting aside so much time each day for prayer, are not bad things.

In fact, they are right and are things that Christians should do. They are things that good Christians definitely will do. Therefore, these things that are good are not made death to us. So, what is happening here?

Paul is saying that even though the commandments do not bring death, if the believer thinks his efforts in trying to keep the commandments will make him righteous and holy, then his faith is misplaced, and spiritual death will definitely be the result. We can say the same thing as it regards the disciplines that I have just given.

If our faith is placed in those things, even though the things are good within themselves, we will find that sin, that it might appear sin, will work death in us by that which is good (Rom. 7:13).

The problem is not the things we are doing that are good,

but the problem is our misplaced faith. In other words, we are placing faith in those things, thinking that the doing of them makes us holy when that is not the case at all. So, the result is failure, i.e., sin. Now the Christian is left very confused.

UNDERSTANDING

This is the reason that Paul said: *"For that which I do I allow not: for what I would, that do I not; but what I hate, that do I"* (Rom. 7:15).

The word *allow* should have been translated *understand,* for that's what it actually means. It would then read: *"For that which I do I* understand *not."*

What was it that the apostle didn't understand?

He didn't understand why he was failing, considering that he was trying so hard not to fail.

The believer must understand that Romans, Chapter 7, is Paul's experience before he was given the understanding of the Cross. In other words, out of this desperation, the Lord would show him the meaning of the new covenant, which was actually the meaning of the Cross. Paul gives us the meaning of the new covenant in the entirety of his 14 epistles, but especially in Romans, Chapters 6 and 8. So, before he understood the Message of the Cross, which brings victory within one's life, he was trying to live for God by his own efforts. In other words, he was trying to keep the law by his strength and willpower, which he was unable to do. In fact, no one else can either.

WRETCHED MAN

That's why Paul said: *"O wretched man that I am! Who shall deliver me from the body of this death?"* (Rom. 7:24).

So, we have Christians doing all types of good things, thinking that the doing of these things makes them righteous and holy. It doesn't! While the Lord most definitely will bless any believer for all the good things done, whatever they might be, still, that will not make anyone righteous or holy. So, we are not condemning the doing of good things, but rather we are condemning faith placed in those things.

Without fail, our faith must be anchored squarely in Christ and what Christ did at the Cross. It doesn't matter how much the Christian claims to have faith in Christ, if he doesn't understand that it is the Cross that makes possible everything we have from God, then, in reality, his faith is in *"another Jesus"* (II Cor. 11:4).

If our good works are produced by righteousness and holiness, then our reward will be great. If we are trying to produce righteousness and holiness by good works, then we will be on the short end of that proverbial stick. In other words, there won't be any proper reward.

ALPHA AND OMEGA

"I am Alpha and Omega, the beginning and the end, the first and the last" (Rev. 22:13).

The phrase, *"I am Alpha and Omega,"* presents the first

letter in the Greek alphabet (alpha) and the last letter in the Greek alphabet (omega). It is another way of saying, "The first and the last," which includes all in-between.

THE BEGINNING AND THE END

The phrase, *"the beginning and the end,"* says the same thing as *"alpha and omega."*

It doesn't mean that Christ as God had a beginning, for He didn't. Christ as God has always been, always is, and always shall be. When it uses these terms, such as *"the beginning and the end,"* it is speaking of whatever it is in question. In this case, it would be addressing itself to the great salvation process. Salvation began with Christ, and it will end with Christ. So, that means that there is salvation in nothing else, which means that all the religions of the world are bogus.

THE FIRST AND THE LAST

The phrase, *"The first and the last,"* is the same as the other two phrases.

All of this is said for effect so that the reader will have absolutely no misunderstanding of who Jesus actually is.

The repetition of these glorious titles is not a mere idle repetition or designed to give a rhetorical fullness to the proceedings of this book. In fact, the repetition is closely allied with the preceding thought.

Men will answer to Christ! To be sure, and irrespective of whether the world believes it or not, He is coming back to this earth. His reward being with Him signifies that it is to Him that the world will answer. As well, the term *"every man"* guarantees that all will answer! In other words, it means exactly what it says!

BLESSED

"Blessed are they who do His commandments, that they may have the right to the Tree of Life, and may enter in through the gates into the city" (Rev. 22:14).

The phrase, *"Blessed are they,"* presents the seventh and last beatitude in the entirety of the book of Revelation. Those seven are as follows:

1. *"Blessed is he who reads, and they who hear the words of this prophecy, and keep those things which are written therein"* (Rev. 1:3).
2. *"Blessed are the dead which die in the Lord from henceforth"* (Rev. 14:13).
3. *"Blessed is he who watches, and keeps his garments"* (Rev. 16:15).
4. *"Blessed are they which are called unto the marriage supper of the Lamb"* (Rev. 19:9).
5. *"Blessed and holy is he who has part in the first resurrection"* (Rev. 20:6).
6. *"Blessed is he who keeps the sayings of the prophecy of this book"* (Rev. 22:7).
7. *"Blessed are they who have washed their robes in the blood of the Lamb"* (Rev. 22:14).

We will find here that the blessing promised as it regards this last beatitude is glorious beyond compare. In fact, the blessings of the Lord are always of infinite value. Understanding that, we should want and desire those blessings more than anything else.

Blessed in the Greek is *makarios* and means "fortunate, well-off, happy."

THE BLOOD OF THE LAMB

The phrase, *"who do His commandments,"* should have been translated, *"Who wash their robes in the blood of the Lamb."*

The Greek text used for the King James Version of the Bible was the Textus Receptus. It is the text that Erasmus, the famous Renaissance scholar, published in A.D. 1516. It was the first New Testament Greek text ever published. It contains the statement, *"Blessed are they that do His commandments,"* but that's not the way that John originally wrote it.

He originally said, *"Blessed are they who wash their robes in the blood of the Lamb."*

So, why was it changed?

It was evidently changed by a particular scribe, whomever he may have been, because he said to himself that no man can be saved just by trusting Jesus. One cannot go to heaven and enter through those beautiful gates just by washing his robes in the blood of the Lamb. "A man has to earn heaven," said that particular scribe to himself. So, the scribe took upon himself the authority to change the statement.

SCHOLARSHIP AND ARCHEOLOGY

Since 1516, the world of scholarship and archeology has discovered thousands of earlier Greek texts. In fact, there are presently over 4,000 Greek manuscripts of the New Testament, with each manuscript containing all the books of the New Testament or portions of the books.

Besides this overwhelming collection in Greek, scholars have discovered more than 8,000 Latin versions and more than 1,000 other versions of the New Testament, with some of them going back to as early as A.D. 300.

By comparing these thousands and thousands of manuscripts, the scholars can easily find the original text the apostle wrote. The overwhelming evidence is that in this particular passage, he said, *"Blessed are they who wash their robes in the blood of the Lamb, that they may have right to the Tree of Life, and may enter in through the gates into the city."*

So, once again, we come back to the question of why did this particular scribe change the gospel message from one of faith and trust to one of obedience and works.

The answer is simple! There is the everlasting tendency in a man to try to merit, to try to achieve, or to try by self-advancement to find his way into heaven. That is a weakness of human nature, and it is seen everywhere in religion.

THE DOCTRINE OF MERIT

Regarding the following, I quote W. A. Criswell:

This system of merit represents the great religions of the world. It represents much of Christianity. Many churches in Christendom believe that we are saved by works, that a man toils his way into the kingdom of heaven, that he deserves heaven as a reward after he has done certain things that he thinks are acceptable unto God. Certainly the great religions, like the Hindu, the Confucian, and the Buddhist, are religions of works. A Hindu will keep his hand raised up toward heaven until it becomes stiff, or he will lie on a bed of hot coals or spikes, or he will crawl on his knees from one city to a shrine miles away, seeking to deserve the pardon of God.

This same kind of merit system is seen in the Christian faith as well. So much of Christianity is built around the doctrine of trying to deserve the favor of heaven. A man is saved, says one preacher, by trusting in Jesus and by being baptized. Another preacher says a man is saved by trusting Jesus and doing all kinds of good works. Another says a man is saved by believing in Jesus and taking the Lord's Supper. Another says a man is saved by trusting in the Lord Jesus and becoming a member of the church and by being obedient to all of the commandments of the church.

The doctrine of merit is a reflection of human pride. The falsely proud, conceited man says: 'I can do this assignment myself. I can merit heaven myself. I can work out this problem of sin by myself. And when I am saved, it is because I have done it. Look at me. Here I am walking golden streets, going through gates of pearl, mingling with the saints of God because I did good, I obeyed commandments, I kept laws, and I did great things. Therefore am I here in the presence of God.'

That is the religion of the flesh; that is the religion of human pride; and that was the religion of the scribe who, when he found this passage in Revelation, changed the text from one of washing robes in the blood of the Lamb, to one of doing commandments.

SIN

Keeping commandments, or at least our thinking that we keep them, can never cleanse one single sin. In fact, all the good things we might do, as helpful as they might be, and as commendable as they might be, can never cleanse from sin. If one thinks about it just a moment, it becomes crystal clear that works cannot cleanse from sin.

The idea behind a works religion is that we owe a debt, and the works that we perform pay that debt. Unfortunately, our thinking is way off.

It's like trying to pay a $1 billion debt with a few pennies. It simply cannot be done.

Sin cannot be cleansed in that manner and cannot be cleansed at all. While sin is definitely a debt, it is far more than a debt. It is a bondage and an enslavement, and it carries with it a power that must be addressed, which cannot be done merely by payment.

For instance, all the money in the world cannot cure cancer or AIDS. You could stack $100 bills all over a person afflicted with these diseases, and it would do no good. You could, in fact, pay any amount of money, and the payment of such would have no effect on these diseases.

For these diseases to be affected in a positive way, which means to be cured, there has to be a medicine that is stronger than the disease, which will kill the germs that are causing the affliction. Money cannot do that, or any type of works for that matter.

THE PRICE

It is the same with sin! It is definitely true that Jesus paid the price. The price that He paid made it possible not only for God to wipe the slate clean, in other words, to erase the debt, but it also made it possible for the Holy Spirit to attack the very source of sin.

That's why Paul said, *"But if the Spirit (Holy Spirit) of Him (God the Father) who raised up Jesus from the dead dwell in you, He who raised up Christ from the dead shall also quicken your mortal bodies by His Spirit who dwells in you"* (Rom. 8:11).

Sin is a spiritual problem and has to be addressed by spiritual means, which is the Cross of Christ and the Holy Spirit.

The cause of sin is a diseased, polluted, unregenerate,

blasphemous, wicked, and ungodly heart. I realize that most people do not like to think of themselves in that vein, but what I've said is correct. That can only be changed by regeneration, and regeneration can only be brought about by what Jesus did at the Cross and our faith in that finished work (Jn. 3:16; Rom. 5:1-2; 6:3-14; 8:1-2, 11; Col. 2:14-15; Eph. 2:8-9, 12-18).

The forgiveness and cleansing of sin lies strictly in the mercy, goodness, love, compassion, and forbearance of God. All the burnt offerings in the world and all the commandments that a man can keep can never suffice to blot out the stain of sin in his soul.

The prophet said: *"Ho, everyone who thirsts* (is thirsty), *come you to the waters, and he who has no money; come you, buy, and eat; yes, come, buy wine and milk without money and without price .... Incline your ear, and come unto Me: hear, and your soul shall live"* (Isa. 55:1-3).

ABRAHAM

How was Abraham justified?

If Abraham was justified by works, he then would have room to boast. In that event, the Patriarch could say: "Look what I have done. I have merited salvation, and I deserve heaven." However, Paul avowed that Abraham could not boast before God, for God knew his heart as He knows our hearts.

Listen to this: You can take the sweetest, purest, and finest girl in the world, and put on a screen all the secrets of her heart and of her life, and she will blush with indescribable shame. That is the same with every human being. That's the reason the Scripture says that all have sinned and come short of the glory of God. No person, that is, if he is in his right mind, can boast before God. So, how was Abraham justified?

The Scripture plainly says: *"Abraham believed God, and it was counted unto Him for righteousness"* (Rom. 4:3).

Then the Holy Spirit through Paul said: *"But to him who works not* (depends not on works), *but believes on Him who justifies the ungodly, his faith is counted for righteousness"* (Rom. 4:5).

This is the only way that a human being can be saved. It is altogether by faith, and more particularly, faith in Christ and what Christ has done for us at the Cross. If we try to come any other way, we automatically shoot ourselves down, so to speak. In fact, our works of righteousness in God's sight are as filthy rags (Isa. 64:6).

It is *"not by works of righteousness which we have done, but according to His mercy He saved us, by the washing of regeneration"* (Titus 3:5).

MARTIN LUTHER

The great Protestant Reformation came about over this very thing—this doctrinal difference.

There was a monk by the name of Martin Luther, who attended the services of St. John Lateran's Church in Rome.

In front of the church of St. John Lateran is a building,

housing what is called "Scala Santa," the Holy Stairs. It is supposed to be the same set of stairs up which the Lord Jesus walked into the judgment hall of Pontius Pilate. On the stairway are supposed to be the blood drops of the Lord Jesus.

In order to preserve the stairs and the blood drops, the stairs are covered with wood with little glass holes to exhibit the blood drops. As people climb the stairway on their knees, they kiss those little glass holes where the blood drops of Jesus are supposed to be. This is supposed to merit them something as it regards salvation, etc.

So, in order to achieve salvation, or whatever it is they desire, the people climb up those steps, hour after hour, trying to work their way into the kingdom of God by penance.

Martin Luther was doing that. He was climbing those same stairs, kissing all those spots, when about halfway up, something happened in his heart. He recalled the great text of Habakkuk 2:4: *"The just shall live by his faith."*

It is said that Martin Luther stood up, turned around, and walked down the steps. He went to Wittenberg, Germany, and there on the door of the church, he nailed his Ninety-Five Theses, and that was the beginning of the Reformation.

No, the words that John wrote are: *"Blessed are they who have washed their robes in the blood of the Lamb, that they may have the right to the Tree of Life, and may enter in through the gates into the city"* (Rev. 22:14).

"For by grace are you saved through faith; and that not of yourselves: it is the gift of God: Not of works, lest any man should boast" (Eph. 2:8-9).

THE TREE OF LIFE

The phrase, *"that they may have the right to the Tree of Life,"* proclaims the fact that this right can be attained in only one way, and that is by washing our robes in the blood of the Lamb, i.e., trusting in Christ and what He did for us at the Cross.

To be frank, what we are addressing here is the very heart of the gospel. What is it that gives us the right to claim Christ, to claim salvation, or to claim a home in heaven?

We maintain that there is only one thing that gives us that right, and that is what our Lord did at the Cross and our faith in that finished work. What He did at the Cross was all done on our behalf. We believe this and this alone is the passport to the great privilege of being born again (Jn. 3:3). It is the blood of Jesus Christ alone that cleanses from all sin (I Jn. 1:7).

Ellicott said, "The best who have striven and conquered were victors not by their own might, but by the blood of the Lamb" (Rev. 12:11).

THE GATES INTO THE CITY

The phrase, *"and may enter in through the gates into the city,"* proclaims the eternal abode of the redeemed. The right to live in this city, and to live there forever, is strictly because of the grace of God. The means of this grace is the Cross of Christ. It is attained by faith.

In retrospect, the commandments of God are definitely to be kept; however, if we set out to keep the commandments by using any tactic at our disposal, we will fail every single time.

The Lord Jesus Christ has already kept all the commandments and did so perfectly. In fact, He did this in His earthly life simply because we couldn't do it for ourselves.

He also addressed the commandments that had been broken by every single human being, and He did so by paying the full penalty by giving His life on the Cross.

When we come to Christ and make Him our Lord and Saviour, in the mind of God, we are literally placed *"in Christ"* (Rom. 8:1). Consequently, His victory becomes our victory. His perfect obedience becomes our perfect obedience.

Listen to what Paul said: *"I am crucified with Christ: nevertheless I live; yet not I, but Christ lives in me: and the life which I now live in the flesh I live by the faith of the Son of God, who loved me, and gave Himself for me"* (Gal. 2:20).

In this one passage, Paul tells us that he lives this life by the faith of the Son of God, which refers to what Christ did for us at the Cross and our faith in that sacrifice.

In essence, he said that if he does not try to live this life in that manner, which refers to all the commandments being kept, but tries to do it another way, he will *"frustrate the grace of God"* (Gal. 2:21).

Most definitely, we are supposed to keep all of the commandments; however, the only way this can be done is by Christ living through us and in us. He does this through the power and person of the Holy Spirit. He functions in our lives totally and completely within the parameters of what Christ did at the Cross and our faith in that finished work. The

Bible definitely demands obedience, but it's obedience in the realm of Christ and never obedience in the sense of our own works, etc.

WITHOUT

"For without are dogs, and sorcerers, and whoremongers, and murderers, and idolaters, and whosoever loves and makes a lie" (Rev. 22:15).

From all of this, we learn that Jesus saves *from* sin and not *in* sin. In fact, the basic foundation of the gospel is the changed life.

Claiming that we are saved but then continuing on in these types of sins listed here makes bogus such claims. Those who practice such sins will not have the right to the Tree of Life or to enter in through the gates into the city.

Incidentally, the *"dogs"* listed here are not the canine variety, but rather homosexuals.

DOGS

The phrase, *"For without are dogs,"* refers to homosexuals.

"You shall not bring the hire of a whore, or the price of a dog (homosexual), *into the house of the* Lord *your God for any vow: for even both these are abomination unto the* Lord *your God"* (Deut. 23:18).

In Hebrew, the word *dog* is *keleb.* It means a male prostitute, homosexual, or sodomite.

SORCERERS

The phrase, *"and sorcerers,"* has to do with all types of witchcraft, incantations, spirits, and fortune-telling.

WHOREMONGERS

The phrase, *"and whoremongers,"* pertains to all types of immorality. Actually, this is the great sin of the present age. Immorality is rampant. It is so rampant, in fact, that almost half of the babies born in this nation are born out of wedlock.

MURDERERS

The phrase, *"and murderers,"* pertains not only to killing in cold blood but, as well, murdering one's reputation through gossip, etc.

IDOLATRY

The phrase, *"and idolaters,"* pertains to placing anything above God or on a par with God. To be frank, idolatry is one of the most oft committed sins. Millions claim that in order to be saved, one has to belong to his or her particular church. This is idolatry! Others claim that water baptism must be joined to faith in Christ. This is idolatry! As one can see, the list is long!

To escape this sin, we must place our faith exclusively in Christ and what Christ has done for us at the Cross (Jn. 3:16; I Cor. 2:2).

LIARS

The phrase, *"and whosoever loves and makes a lie,"* refers to anything that's untrue.

We are being told here that we cannot live a life of sin and expect to gain the rewards of salvation.

WITHOUT

The term *"without"* is meant to refer to eternal hell. The idea is that the person is not merely outside the New Jerusalem; he is confined to eternal hell, and confined there forever and forever.

Never be sad or desponding,
If you have faith to believe,
Grace, for the duties before thee,
Ask of your God and receive.

What if your burdens oppress thee;
What though your life may be drear;
Look on the side that is brightest,
Pray, and your path will be clear.

Never be sad or desponding,
There is a morrow for thee;
Soon you shall dwell in its brightness,
There with the Lord you shall be.

Never be sad or desponding,
Lean on the arm of your Lord,
Dwell in the depths of His mercy,
You shall receive your reward.

THE NEW JERUSALEM

C H A P T E R 5

THE BRIGHT AND
MORNING STAR

CHAPTER FIVE

THE BRIGHT AND
MORNING STAR

"I JESUS HAVE SENT My angel to testify unto you these things in the churches. I am the root and the offspring of David, and the bright and morning star" (Rev. 22:16).

JESUS

Jesus appears here as the speaker, ratifying and confirming all that has been communicated through the entirety of this book.

Angel here means "messenger"; consequently, the pastors, for that is to whom it refers, are to testify these things in the churches.

Jesus is the root and the offspring of David, which refers to the incarnation. He is, as well, the King who will sit on the Davidic throne. This also speaks of the Cross.

Christ is also the bright and morning star, meaning that Satan isn't!

The short phrase, *"I Jesus,"* is found only here in Scripture, emphasizing its importance. This means that Christ is here closing out the account of what has been said, but most of all,

He is testifying to the truth of that which has been given. It is not merely a message or the confirmation of a message that we have, but rather the root and pledge of hope to all. These words given by Christ authenticate all that has been said. Any method of interpreting these visions that blunts the application of the message does so over these words of Christ.

The whole book of Revelation is a message to the churches. Therefore, any method of interpreting Revelation that blunts the application of this message in its entirety to the present church does so in the spirit of apostasy.

THE CHURCHES

The phrase, *"have sent My angel to testify unto you these things in the churches,"* is meant to proclaim the fact that the Lord intends for all believers to know and understand this that is given. Consequently, even though it may take a little time, if we are ignorant of what is stated in these visions, then the ignorance is willful ignorance. The reason for the information given concerning the New Jerusalem is that we might know what the eternal future of the redeemed might be. It's a beautiful picture.

If it is to be noticed, the word *churches* is used in the plural. This means that the Lord is going to deal with every church according to the way that it has allowed the light to shine or has stifled that light. This means that each church will answer, and, in essence, each pastor will answer. Each one will answer to Christ and not some denominational hierarchy. Every preacher of the gospel had best read these words very, very carefully.

THE ROOT OF DAVID

The phrase, *"I am the root and the offspring of David,"* is meant to project, as stated, the incarnation of Christ. The Lord is reminding us that He became man and suffered all the privations of man that we might be saved. As a man—*the* Man Christ Jesus—He overcame Satan, and He did so at the Cross. As a man full of the Holy Spirit, He healed the sick and cast out demons. As a man, He went to the Cross where He poured out His life's blood and, thereby, redeemed humanity. As a man, He was buried in a tomb, and as a man, He arose from the dead on the third day. As the Man Christ Jesus, He today sits at the right hand of the Father making intercession for the saints (Heb. 7:25).

In II Samuel, Chapter 7, the Lord told David that it would be through his family that the Messiah would come. To be sure, this was and is an honor of unprecedented proportions. I speak of it being an honor for David!

Christ is David's Lord and David's Son, possessing David's throne (Mat. 22:42-45; Lk. 1:32). Jesus Christ is the Messiah of Israel, but He is also the Saviour of the world (Jn. 3:16).

Ironically enough, the name of David is the first human name mentioned in the New Testament (Mat. 1:1) and the last human name mentioned in the New Testament (Rev. 22:16).

THE BRIGHT AND MORNING STAR

The phrase, *"and the bright and morning star,"* refers to

the fact that in Christ, the new day is about to dawn. In this manner, He is the morning star.

He said to the overcomer at Thyatira, *"I will give him the morning star"* (Rev. 2:28). Back in Numbers 24:17, it says, *"There shall come a star out of Jacob."*

In a physical sense, the term applies to several of the planets, but more particularly, to Venus because of its superior luster. As morning stars, they shine brightest if and when the moon has set in the west, that is, when neither sun nor moon is in the sky. At that time, the morning star appears. It is the star that precedes the rising of the sun and leads on the day.

Perhaps the reference here is to that star as the harbinger of day, and the meaning of the Saviour is that He sustains a relation to a dark world similar to this beautiful star. He is also compared with the sun itself in giving light to the world. Here He is compared with that morning star rather with reference to its beauty than its light.

A NEW BEGINNING

Concerning this star, Barnes says: "May it not also have been one object in this comparison to lead us, when we look on that star, to think of the Saviour? It is perhaps the most beautiful object in nature; it succeeds the darkness of the night; it brings on the day—and as it mingles with the first rays of the morning, it seems to be so joyous, cheerful, exulting, bright, that nothing can be better adapted to remind us of Him who came to lead an eternal day."

As well, and as should by now be obvious, *"morning star"* speaks of a new beginning. Mankind is mired in sin with a life of the past leaning more toward waste than anything else. The *"morning star"* is telling man that in Christ, one can begin again. One can have a brand-new start—a brand-new day, but it's only in Christ that such can be!

Greater yet, it doesn't matter how bad the situation is, the morning star says, "I can help you begin again! I can make you what you ought to be!"

Oh, dear reader, can you not sense the presence of God even as you read these words? The message is to you! It is His love for you regardless of the past or the present. He loves you and is telling you, "I am the bright and morning star!"

And so He is.

THE GREAT INVITATION

"And the Spirit and the bride say, Come. And let him who hears say, Come. And let him who is athirst come. And whosoever will, let him take the water of life freely" (Rev. 22:17).

The phrase, *"And the Spirit and the bride say, Come,"* presents the cry of the Holy Spirit to a hurting, lost, and dying world and, as well, the cry of all the redeemed who make up the bride. The message is simple, so simple, in fact, that even a child can understand what is being said—*"Come!"*

That is the great invitation. The wonderful thing about this is that it has no qualifiers. There is no discrimination. As it opens the door wide to any sinner, it opens the door wide to the vilest of sinners. This is a plea from the heart of God: *"Come!"*

It is that men may come to the Saviour; they may come and partake of the blessings of the gospel; and they may come and be saved. Nothing is more appropriate to this book than to announce in the clearest and most concise way that salvation is free to all, and that whosoever will may come and be saved.

If it is to be noticed, the Holy Spirit and the redeemed are joined here. This means, at least presently, that if the church is in tune with the Holy Spirit and is properly hearing what the Spirit is saying to the churches, the emphasis will be on the presentation of the gospel message to a hurting world. Everything else must be secondary.

This is at least one of the reasons that my heart bleeds at much of the church today, which chases a gospel that is not really the gospel. In other words, it could be construed as blasphemy!

If we, the redeemed, do not have the words of life, then who does? I can assure you that the politicians don't, and neither do the educators, the psychologists, the sociologists, or anyone else for that matter. It's only those who have been redeemed by the blood of the Lamb who can tell others of Jesus and what He has done for all of us by the giving of His life on the Cross.

There is no one else in the world saying, "Come," at least as it refers to the Saviour. That means that it's our task as the redeemed to get this job done. This is what the Spirit is saying, and it is what we must be saying.

JESUS

We must make certain that the Jesus we are preaching is not another Jesus, projected by another spirit, which presents another gospel (II Cor. 11:4).

While it must be Jesus we bring to a hurting world, we must make doubly certain that the Jesus we hold up and present is, in fact, *"Jesus Christ, and Him crucified"* (I Cor. 2:2).

If it is to be noticed, Paul said, *"But we preach Christ crucified"* (I Cor. 1:23).

He did not merely say, "We preach Christ," but rather, *"We preach Christ crucified."* There is a vast difference in the two statements!

The apostle also said, *"For after that in the wisdom of God the world by wisdom knew not God, it pleased God by the foolishness of preaching* (preaching the Cross) *to save them who believe"* (I Cor. 1:21).

So, when we say, "Come to Jesus," we must understand that it is His Cross that makes it possible for man to be saved. In other words, every single thing the human being receives from God comes exclusively through the Cross, which means that this is where our faith must be anchored (Rom. 6:3-14; 8:1-2, 11).

There are some who claim that the phrase, *And the Spirit and the bride say, Come,"* refers to the return of Christ and is not meant to be an evangelistic appeal.

While it is undoubtedly the cry of the Spirit and the bride for the imminent return of our Lord, still, the tenor of the verse leans heavily toward an evangelistic appeal. It appeals to the one who is thirsty, which, of course, speaks of a spiritual thirst. It tells him to take the water of life freely. Nothing could be clearer or plainer. Pure and simple, this is an evangelistic appeal and, in fact, the greatest evangelistic appeal found in the entirety of the Word of God. How fitting and appropriate it is to close out the canon of Scripture.

TO HEAR THE GOSPEL

The phrase, *"And let him who hears say, Come,"* refers to the soul who hears the gospel. Paul said: *"How then shall they call on Him in whom they have not believed? and how shall they believe in Him of whom they have not heard? and how shall they hear without a preacher?"* (Rom. 10:14).

Anyone who hears the gospel can say, "Come," because that's exactly what the Holy Spirit is saying. It means that if they can hear, they can come.

It is the business of all the redeemed, symbolized by the bride, to see to it that all have an opportunity to hear. The Holy Spirit places great emphasis on that.

God has already done everything that heaven can do as it regards the salvation of mankind. He has sent His only begotten Son to this world to die on a Cross, making it possible for man to be saved. It's now the business of the church, referred to as the Great Commission, to take this great message to the world. It truly is the greatest story ever told; however, it is great only to those who have the privilege of hearing it. Regrettably, there are many who do not have that privilege. It is the responsibility of all the redeemed, i.e., the bride, to see to it that all do have that privilege.

That's the reason that we are on television all over the world. That's the reason we ask you to pray for us and to support us financially. It is so that we can take this grand story, this eternal message, and this for which such a price has been paid to those who so desperately need it.

ATHIRST

The phrase, *"And let him who is athirst come,"* speaks of spiritual thirst—the cry for God in the soul of man.

There is a void in unredeemed man. It is certainly true that all unredeemed are spiritually dead, which means that they have no desire for God or spiritual things. At least they have no desire for those things that are truly spiritual. Still, the void cries out to be filled. Unredeemed man doesn't know what it is and tries to fill it with the things of this world, which never satisfy, irrespective of what they might be.

The reason is simple: Material things cannot satisfy a spiritual thirst, and that's what that void is. It's actually a thirst for that which is of God. The creation cannot know fulfillment without the Creator.

That's the reason that Jesus clearly said: *"If any man thirst, let him come unto Me, and drink. He who believes on Me, as the Scripture has said, out of his belly* (innermost being) *shall flow rivers of living water"* (Jn. 7:37-38).

As someone has well said, "The soul of man is so big that only God can fill it up." Outside of Christ, that thirst can never be slaked. Outside of Christ, there is no satisfaction. Outside of Christ, the void can never be filled.

THE WATER OF LIFE

The phrase, *"And whosoever will, let him take the water of life freely,"* opens the door to every single individual in the world. Jesus died for all (Jn. 3:16) and, therefore, all can be saved if they will only come.

This one phrase completely shoots down the unscriptural doctrine of predestination, at least in the sense that it is commonly interpreted. I speak of the idea, as claimed by some, that God has already predestined every individual. They say that some are predestined for heaven and some for hell, and they have no choice in the matter. Nothing could be further from the truth!

The clarion cry of the entirety of the Word of God all the way from Genesis 1:1 through Revelation 22:21, in effect, is the cry of the Holy Spirit. It is *"whosoever will!"*

The water of life is available to all, and as the Scripture plainly says, it is free. This echoes the words of Christ: *"Come unto Me, all you who labor and are heavy laden, and I will give you rest"* (Mat. 11:28).

The words *"the water of life"* are a symbolism of the salvation offered by Christ and Christ alone.

ETERNAL LIFE

It all pertains to eternal life, but it carries even greater connotations than that. The very word *life* speaks of all things that are true, honest, right, and straight. Consequently, it's the only thing that will satisfy the cry of the human heart.

Until a person truly finds Christ, that person doesn't know what living actually is. That is true irrespective of whom he might be or how wealthy he might be. And yet, because of the unredeemed being spiritually dead, they have absolutely no inkling of what the Christ-life actually affords. It is a blank to them. In fact, from their vantage point, living for Jesus seems to be the most boring thing that one could ever experience.

With that being the case, how can anyone come to Christ?

THE GOSPEL

The unredeemed must hear the gospel. When the gospel is preached, the Holy Spirit anoints the Word that is sent out and, at the same time, convicts the unredeemed of his or her lost condition. At that moment he begins to realize that his state is not what it ought to be. As the Holy Spirit convicts him, he now has an opportunity to accept Christ. Those who do find a world open to them that they never really knew existed. For the first time, they find a purpose and reason for living. Christ becomes all in all, with life taking on a brand-new meaning. They now see everything differently!

That's what Paul was talking about when the Holy Spirit said through him, *"Therefore if any man be in Christ, he is a new creature* (creation): *old things are passed away; behold, all things are become new"* (II Cor. 5:17).

CHARLES SPURGEON

Charles Spurgeon was one of the great preachers of the gospel in the 19TH century. His church in London touched that city plus, in a measure, the entirety of England.

He came from a family that was quite well-to-do; therefore, he was well educated as a young man.

During that time, he became very concerned about his soul. He joined several churches but to no avail. The hunger, the thirst, and the longing were not satisfied. In other words, the emptiness and the void were not filled.

As the months went by, he became more and more concerned and more and more perturbed, which he attempted to alleviate in various ways but with no success.

One particular night, greatly agitated of soul, he was walking the streets of London. It began to rain, and he sought shelter.

He saw a light ahead, and thinking it was some type of public place, he hurried there to get out of the rain. To his surprise, it was a small mission—a small church.

He walked inside out of the rain, and there were only a few people present. There was a man behind the pulpit preaching, but after a few moments, it was obvious that he was, at the same time, very uneducated, which grated the nerves of Spurgeon. The bad grammar and the halting English did not endear itself to this educated young man.

LOOK TO HIM

The man's subject that night as he was preaching was "Look to Him!"

He didn't have much body to his sermon, so he repeated the phrase over and over, "Look to Him!"

Of course, his theme was Christ, and his petition was that people should come to Christ, and if they did, the thirst of their souls would be satisfied. "Look to Him!"

Those words seized the soul of Spurgeon. Holy Spirit conviction set in. In a few moments, he forgot the bad grammar and the halting English. The uneducated accent ceased to trouble him, with the words, "Look to Him," looming large in his heart.

That night, Charles Haddon Spurgeon found Christ. In that little mission where he said yes to Jesus, the thirst of his soul was completely satisfied, even as it has been satisfied in the hearts and lives of untold millions. In a moment's time, every question was answered! The void was filled! He was born again. The water of life had been offered to him freely, and he had taken it.

Let the reader understand that this man had joined several churches before now, but to no avail. This shows that the church cannot satisfy the longing of the human heart, and neither can anything else. In fact, if the church doesn't preach Jesus and Him crucified, and do so as the constant theme of its existence, then the church is of no consequence. It is Jesus and Jesus alone who can give the water of life. How does He do this grand and glorious thing?

CHRIST CRUCIFIED

Paul said, and as previously stated, *"But we preach Christ crucified"* (I Cor. 1:23).

Why did the great apostle use this term in this fashion?

He did it because the Holy Spirit directed him accordingly.

Someone asked me once, "Is salvation afforded by who Jesus is or what Jesus has done?" signifying the Cross.

Perhaps it's a moot question because it is only Christ who could have done this thing, and we speak of affording salvation, because man certainly could not do such for himself. However, the greater emphasis must always lay on the fact of *what* He did, referring to the Cross.

Jesus Christ is God. As God, He had no beginning, which means that He always was and, in fact, always is. As God, He is unformed, unmade, uncreated, has always been, and always will be, but the simple fact of Him being God, as wonderful, glorious, and necessary as that is, did not save anyone. If that alone could save, then He did not need to leave the throne of glory and take upon Himself the frailty of humanity.

THE INCARNATION

To effect the salvation of mankind, the Cross was an absolute necessity. Due to the fact that God cannot die, God would have to become man.

So, let the reader always remember the following: Jesus as God, by that mere fact alone, did not save anyone. Jesus the miracle worker did not save anyone. Jesus the healer did not save anyone. It was Jesus the Saviour who redeemed lost humanity, and He did so *"by the Cross, having slain the enmity thereby"* (Eph. 2:16). In that way and that way alone could man be reconciled to God. He had to go to the Cross and there shed His life's blood, which atoned for all sin—past, present, and future—at least for all who will believe. This is what made it possible for man to be saved. That's why Paul said, *"We preach Christ crucified."* If the church doesn't preach the Cross (I Cor. 1:21), then the church is not preaching the gospel, which means that no water of life is offered. Sadly, most churches, and I exaggerate not, are offering everything in the world except the water of life. I say that because they aren't preaching Christ and Him crucified, so that means that no matter what else they preach, no lives will be changed.

However, if we preach the Cross, glorious and wonderful things happen. Lives are changed! Bondages of darkness are broken! The sick are healed! These things are done only as we preach the Cross (I Cor. 1:17-18; 2:2; Col. 2:10-15).

THE PROPHECY OF THIS BOOK

"For I testify unto every man who hears the words of the prophecy of this book, If any man shall add unto these things, God shall add unto him the plagues that are written in this book" (Rev. 22:18).

The phrase, *"For I testify unto every man who hears the*

words of the prophecy of this book," proclaims the inerrancy
of these messages. In other words, John testifies that it is the
Word of God.

As well, it is a book of prophecy. Four times it is called that
(Rev. 1:3; 22:10, 18-19).

Concerning this prophecy, it begins by saying: *"Blessed is
he who reads, and they who hear the words of this prophecy"*
(Rev. 1:3). Of the seven beatitudes in this book, this is the
first one.

The book of Revelation comprises God's answer to the
questions of the ages. It tells us what is happening, and what
shall happen. In fact, it takes man into the unending future.

Chapter 1 of the book of Revelation proclaims the revelation of Christ as He appeared to John. Chapters 2 and 3
proclaim the church age, in which we are still living. In fact,
this is the Laodicean period of the church, which speaks of
its apostasy.

The Ephesian period of the church is referred to as the
apostolic church. It was the time of the apostles and ended
at about A.D. 100. Then the Smyrnean period began, which
is referred to as the martyr church. It ended in about A.D. 300.
Many lost their lives under the iron heel of the Roman Empire
of that day. Then we have the Pergamumian time of the church,
which is referred to as the state church. It is when the church
was married to the state, so to speak. This period ended in
about A.D. 500. Then we have the Thyatiran period, referred
to as the papal church, which continues unto this hour. Then
we have the Sardinian period, which is the Reformation

period, beginning in about the year 1400. At this time, we have the great names such as Martin Luther, John Wesley, John Knox, John Calvin, etc. They were calling the people back to the true faith. In a sense, this period continues, as well, unto this hour. Then we have the Philadelphian period in the church, the church of the wide-open door, referred to as the missionary church. It began at about the year 1800 and, as well, continues unto this hour. Then finally, as stated, we have the Laodicean period of the church, referred to as the apostate church, in which we are now living.

APOSTASY

This is the time when the church says of itself, *"I am rich, and increased with goods, and have need of nothing"* (Rev. 3:17).

That is what the church thinks of itself, but what did Jesus say?

"Knowest not that you are wretched, and miserable, and poor, and blind, and naked" (Rev. 3:17).

What an indictment!

I realize that my words will not be eagerly received; however, what we say is the truth. There is apostasy everywhere—in the chairs of theology, in the pulpits, and in the unconcern and indifference of the people.

Most of the denominational world has denied the Holy Spirit, so they are left with nothing but religious machinery, which means there is nothing being done for God in those sectors. Sadly, the Pentecostal world, which, in fact, claims the baptism with the Holy Spirit, for the most part has abandoned the Holy Spirit. It, along with its denominational counterparts, has embraced humanistic psychology, which, in fact, is a vote of no confidence as it regards the Cross. There are some few exceptions in these ranks, but not many.

When I was a boy, the attack against the Cross of Christ was carried out by the modernists. Today it is coming from those who claim to be Spirit-filled. The truth is, they are spirit-filled, but it is not with the Holy Spirit. It is evil spirits, i.e., angels of light.

Paul said: *"For such are false apostles, deceitful workers, transforming themselves into the apostles of Christ. And no marvel; for Satan himself is transformed into an angel of light. Therefore it is no great thing if his ministers* (Satan's ministers) *also be transformed as the ministers of righteousness; whose end shall be according to their works"* (II Cor. 11:13-15).

THE RAPTURE OF THE CHURCH

The rapture of the church could take place at any moment, but the church world as a whole doesn't even believe there will be a rapture. In fact, they have little regard for heaven because this present world is their heaven. The denominational world, as well, little looks for the rapture, with most having no knowledge of that doctrine whatsoever.

To be sure, the Baptists and Methodists of several decades ago definitely believed in the rapture, but no more. In fact, for the most part, their churches are filled with people who really aren't even born again. Regrettably, that is getting to be the same way as it regards the Pentecostal world. The charismatics fall into the same category. Once again I emphasize the fact that this is the Laodicean period—the period of apostasy.

THE CROSS OF CHRIST

I firmly believe that the Cross of Christ is going to be and, in fact, already is the dividing line between the true church and the apostate church. As I've said countless times, this has always been the case; however, I believe the Holy Spirit is going to so emphasize the Cross at this present time that there will be no doubt as to what that dividing line actually is.

In Revelation, Chapters 4 and 5, we have the great vision given to John as it regards the throne of God. It is the portrayal of Jesus taking the book out of the hand of God the Father and opening the seven seals thereof, which begins the great tribulation.

Chapters 6 through 18 proclaim the great tribulation period, which is immediately ahead as it regards the time factor. Chapter 19 records the great second coming. Chapter 20 proclaims the coming kingdom age, along with the loosing of Satan from the bottomless pit at the end of that age, with him lasting only for a short period of time. Then he will be placed into the lake of fire, there to remain forever and forever. At the close of the kingdom age, the great white throne judgment will be conducted, along with the renovation of the heaven and the earth.

Chapters 21 and 22 proclaim the perfect age, which will have no end. These are *"the words of the prophecy of this book."*

PLAGUES

In Revelation 22:18 the phrase, *"If any man shall add unto these things, God shall add unto him the plagues that are written in this book,"* proclaims the fact that the changing of the meaning of the prophecies of this book can bring upon one the judgment of God.

The mention of plagues and of God using such, which He most definitely does, opens the door for all types of such things to come upon those who tamper with the Word of God in the realm of unbelief.

The idea is that God in some way will send plagues, even at this very hour. In other words, these things are not reserved only for the coming great tribulation period. On a smaller scale, many and varied things can take place presently and, in fact, do take place presently.

For instance, it is my personal belief that the disease of AIDS is one of these plagues now being sent on the earth because of the great sins of homosexuality, witchcraft, and idolatry practiced presently by so many people.

As well, individuals can cut their lives short or can bring upon themselves various different judgments by ignoring the Word of God.

Along with this word given by John as it regards the book of Revelation, our Lord has said the same thing: *"The Scripture cannot be broken"* (Jn. 10:35).

Moses said: *"You shall not add unto the word ... Neither shall you diminish ought from it"* (Deut. 4:2; 12:32).

Solomon said, *"Add thou not unto His words, lest He reprove you, and you be found a liar"* (Prov. 30:6).

UNBELIEF

John is not speaking here of interpreting the book of Revelation, for many may have different thoughts regarding interpretation, and, in fact, many do. He is primarily speaking of unbelief.

The object is to guard this book against being corrupted by any interpolation or change. Against this danger, John would guard this work in the most solemn manner. Perhaps he felt that as this book would be necessarily regarded as obscure from the fact that symbols were used so much, there was great danger that changes would be made by individuals with a view to making it appear more easily understood, etc.

The book of Revelation, which, of course, proclaims the coming New Jerusalem, was given exactly as the Holy Spirit wanted it to be given. He means for us to study its contents and ask the Lord to help us understand what is being said. It is a picture of the present and the future, and it will not be changed.

Consequently, I would pray that our effort of explanation and manner of interpretation will help you to better understand this prophecy that closes out the canon of Scripture. If that is the case, then we give the Lord all of the praise and all of the glory.

UNBELIEF OF THE WORD OF GOD

"And if any man shall take away from the words of the book of this prophecy, God shall take away his part out of the book of life, and out of the holy city, and from the things which are written in this book" (Rev. 22:19).

The phrase, *"And if any man shall take away from the words of the book of this prophecy,"* proclaims the opposite of the previous verse, which speaks of adding to the words of the prophecy. As should be overly obvious, the idea is that the words of the prophecy should not be changed in any manner, whether addition or deletion.

Williams says, to which we have already alluded: "The sufficiency of the Holy Scriptures as a full and final revelation from God is here asserted in Verses 18 and 19 by the Lord Jesus Himself; and the doom of eternal judgment is denounced upon all who shall add to or subtract from them. While 'this book' means the apocalypse, the warning applies to all Scripture as given by inspiration of God."

Every facet of the Word of God must be taken most seriously. Inasmuch as it is the Word of God, and we speak of the entirety of the canon of Scripture, we must realize that even every single word is important. This is the reason that Jesus said in His answer to Satan, *"It is written, Man shall not live by bread alone, but by every word that proceeds out of the mouth of God"* (Mat. 4:4).

However, when we speak of every word, this does not preclude the changing of words that have grown obsolete to that which is presently used and means the same thing.

Let it be understood that if any believer will sincerely ask the Lord to help him understand the Scriptures, to be sure, the Holy Spirit will guarantee the answer to such a prayer. As well, we should constantly ask the Lord for Him to help us that we not be led astray by our own inclinations and emotions of the flesh. He will answer that prayer also!

I must take the opportunity here to recommend to the reader The Expositor's Study Bible. I personally believe there is no study Bible in the world that will help one understand the Word as this Bible. Incidentally, it is the King James Version.

THE BOOK OF LIFE

The phrase, *"God shall take away his part out of the book of life, and out of the holy city, and from the things which are written in this book,"* presents a solemn warning!

The unredeemed do not bother to study the book of Revelation, or any part of the Bible for that matter. So, it is to be understood that the Holy Spirit here through John is speaking to those who claim Christ.

The solemn warning is given that if men add to this prophecy or take away from this prophecy, God will remove their names from the Book of Life. This means that they are no longer a part of the redeemed and, consequently, have no part in the Holy City. One cannot have one's name removed from the book when it's not there to begin with. So, this simple statement completely shoots down the unscriptural doctrine of unconditional eternal security. We should remember that!

Man has no choice about coming into the world, but after he is here and old enough to be responsible, he is held accountable for his salvation or damnation.

The words *choose* and *will* are used in hundreds of Scriptures, and not one suggests that God forces any man to accept Him and do His will. Man's relationship with God is entirely on a voluntary basis.

FREE MORAL AGENCY

No man recognizing that endless decisions are necessary to daily life can deny the fact of free acts and conduct. To a degree, man has freedom of action—moral action—concerning right and wrong. He is responsible to God for his every act.

It is by his free will that he makes a decision to come to Christ, with, of course, the moving and operation of the Holy Spirit upon his soul. Without the moving and operation of the Holy Spirit, he is unable to favorably respond; however, he is, at the same time, free to respond unfavorably, which many, if not most, actually do.

After salvation, one's free moral agency is certainly not restricted and, in fact, if possible, is strengthened. So, if a person desires to add to or take away from the words of this prophecy, even though the Holy Spirit will deal with him to not do so, he still can carry out such an action and, in fact, many have. With that being the case, and if the individual remains in that state, then God shall take away his part out of the Book of Life. In fact, the entirety of the book of Hebrews was written in regard to this very thing.

AN EVIL DOCTRINE

Many Jews, who had definitely come to Christ, been born again, and even baptized with the Holy Spirit, had now become disconcerted and were either going back into temple worship or seriously considering doing so. To do so, even though they had definitely been saved, would be a denial of Christ and all that He had done at the Cross. This would cause such a person to be eternally lost, that is, if he did this thing and stayed in that particular position of rebellion, denial, and unbelief (Heb. 6:4-6; 10:26-29).

The doctrine of unconditional eternal security is an evil doctrine. It makes millions of people believe that they are saved when, in reality, they aren't. In fact, there are millions in hell right now who are there simply because somebody told them that irrespective of the life they lived, they couldn't lose their salvation. They found to their bitter dismay that those words were not true.

GRACE

Some may argue that we are promoting works. No, we are rather promoting grace, but it's the type of grace that changes one's life. A gospel that effects no change in a person is really not the gospel. The grace of God changes people. That's the reason that John clearly wrote: *"For without are dogs* (homosexuals)*, and sorcerers, and whoremongers, and murderers, and idolaters, and whosoever loves and makes a lie"* (Rev. 22:15).

That's the reason that Paul said, even after naming many particular types of sins, *"Of the which I tell you before, as I have also told you in time past, that they which do such things shall not inherit the kingdom of God"* (Gal. 5:19-21).

Paul is not saying, and neither is John, that those guilty of these sins cannot be forgiven, cleansed, and made new creations in Christ Jesus. In fact, that's the very heart of the gospel. However, these two apostles are definitely saying that the Christian must not think that he can practice a lifestyle of such sins and continue to retain his relationship with Christ. Everything in the gospel militates against such thinking and action.

The Bible doesn't teach sinless perfection, but it definitely does teach victory over sin (Rom. 6:14).

THE CROSS OF CHRIST

Let the reader carefully consider the following: There is a way to live for God and, in fact, only one way. It is as follows:

- Everything we receive from God, irrespective of what it might be, comes by and through Jesus Christ as the source (Jn. 1:1-3, 12; 10:10; 14:6, 20).

- With Jesus as the source, the Cross of Christ is the means by which all of these good things are given to us (Rom. 6:1-14; I Cor. 1:17-18, 23; 2:2).

- With our Lord as the source and the Cross as the means, we must be sure that the Cross of Christ is ever the object of our faith. Of course, we aren't speaking of the wooden beam on which Jesus died, but rather what He there accomplished, which was all by and through the Cross (Col. 2:10-15; Gal. 6:14).

- With our Lord as the source, the Cross as the means, and the Cross as the object of our faith, then the Holy Spirit will go to work on our behalf. Because He is God, He can do anything, but He works exclusively by and through the Cross of Christ. It is the Cross of Christ that gave and gives the Holy Spirit the legal means to do all that He does. However, without our faith in Christ and the Cross, this ties the hands, so to speak, of the Holy Spirit (Rom. 8:1-11; Eph. 2:13-18).

What we have just given you is the way and manner in which the believer is to live for God. If we try to do such any other way, we will fail.

THE WORD OF GOD AND UNBELIEF

As it regards the Christian, every wrong direction, all unbelief, and every disobedience and rebellion against God in any way or manner can be traced back every single time to a misunderstanding or willful misinterpretation of the Word of God. In other words, if we fail, we are missing the Word in some manner. If one will look back over his life, one will see this played out in totality.

The greatest problem with the child of God is a failure to understand the sanctification process and the manner in which the Cross of Christ plays into that process. Perhaps it would be better to say that the sanctification process plays into the Cross of Christ. Most Christians have an understanding of the Cross as it refers to the initial salvation experience; however, as it regards sanctification, most don't have the foggiest idea about what we are speaking. This is sad when we consider that there is nothing more important for the child of God.

In fact, it is impossible for the Christian to live a victorious, overcoming, Christian life without understanding the Cross of Christ as it regards his everyday walk before the Lord. Not understanding the Cross, such a Christian will attempt to live this life by his own efforts, strength, and machinations, which, without fail, brings failure. He will do this every single time.

So, if we don't understand this part of the Word, which, in fact, makes up all of Paul's 14 epistles, then it is for certain that the sin nature is going to rule us and cause all types of problems for the believer. The Cross is the only answer to this dilemma. It is not one of several answers; it is the only answer.

THE TESTIMONY

"He which testifies these things says, Surely I come quickly. Amen. Even so, come, Lord Jesus" (Rev. 22:20).

The phrase, *"He which testifies these things,"* proclaims the fact that the office of the Messiah as Saviour is repeated again and again throughout the prophecy. Williams said, "He is the Lamb that was slain, and His blood washes from sin and alone makes fit for entrance into the eternal city."

In essence, the entire book of Revelation is regarded as the revelation of Jesus Christ to mankind; consequently, He bears witness to the truth of all these things. He speaks here of Himself and vouches for the truth and reality of all that is said by saying that He testifies of them and bears witness to them. The fact that Jesus Himself vouches for the truth of what is revealed here shows the propriety of what John had said in the previous verses about adding to these prophecies or taking from them.

THE SECOND COMING

George Williams said:

The phrase, 'says, Surely I come quickly,' leaves the promise to come as the last message from the Lord Jesus to the believer's heart; and on this sweet note the prophecy ends. The great theme of the New Testament at its opening is the first advent, and its great theme at the close is the second advent. Jesus is coming again! He will ultimately rule this world sitting on the throne of David, and will do so forever. The eternal permanence of restored paradise is assured by the title of Alpha and Omega of Verse 13, for that declares that the Messiah is the one and only God and that there will never be another. The world sees and can see nothing of these coming glories, but to faith the dawn is there, and Christ is the morning star—and more, the bright and morning star to all who love His appearing. His promise to come is the delight and joy of the heart that watches for Him. The world will never know Him as the bright and morning star. All on earth is failure and corruption; but the promise of His coming sustains the faith and strengthens the courage of His people; and animates them to urge whosoever will to take the water of life freely.

COME, LORD JESUS

The phrase, *"Amen. Even so, come, Lord Jesus,"* proclaims the answer of the true church to the promise of Christ regarding the second coming.

The words as given by John present the utterance of desire in the precise language that the Saviour had used—heart responding to heart.

Wrapped up in this one word—*come*—as uttered by John is the exclamation, in a sense, of all that is wrong with this world, and that Jesus Christ alone is its cure, and its only cure. How so true that is!

There will be no solution to the problem of poverty over much of this world until Jesus comes! There will be no solution to the problems of disease that run rampant, decimating entire countries, until Jesus comes! There will be no solution to the race problem until Jesus comes! There will be no solution to the economic crisis that seems to affect the majority of the world time and time again until Jesus comes! There will be no solution to the problem of war and rumors of war until Jesus comes! There will be no solution to the crime problem until Jesus comes! There certainly will be no solution to the problem of sin, which is the cause of all of these problems mentioned, until Jesus comes! As the rapture of the church is the hope of the church, likewise, the second coming is the hope of the world.

WHAT IS THE PRESENT MESSAGE OF THE CHURCH?

I will begin the answer to the question of this subheading by stating what the message of the church ought to be. Jesus said, *"He who has an ear, let him hear what the Spirit says unto the churches"* (Rev. 2:7, 11, 17, 29; 3:6, 13, 22).

What is the Spirit saying to the churches?

The Holy Spirit is proclaiming to the churches all over the world the Message of the Cross. The church came in on the Cross, and the church will go out on the Cross, and I speak of the true church. Is the Message of the Cross that which the modern church is preaching?

Regrettably and sadly, that is not what the modern church is preaching. All of this has to do with the second coming. As stated, the church came in on the Cross and will leave out on the Cross, and that time is very, very near.

One self-anointed prophet (so-called) said the other day that Jesus isn't coming back for 200 or 300 more years simply because His children are having such a good time down here. What utter nonsense! What gross stupidity! It's prattle such as that which is aired over much of what is called Christian television. God help us!

Anyone who is truly saved, and above all, truly Spirit-filled, expresses the same cry that John the Beloved expressed so long ago: *"Amen. Even so, come, Lord Jesus."* Of course, I'm talking about being filled with the Holy Spirit and not spirits. That person knows and understands that the problems of this world are not going to be solved until Jesus comes back.

That person also knows that it's not the purpose of the church in this world to have a good time, but rather to take the glorious message of redemption to a hurting and dying world. When the Spirit and the bride say *"Come,"* how can we do less? If we have heard ourselves, how can we do less than tell those who have not heard to come? We must tell the thirsty that Jesus alone can slake that thirst. We must hold the banner high and say, "Whosoever will, let him take the water of life freely." That is our burden, our mission, our calling, and our purpose. When we leave that, which means that we are no longer abiding in Christ, we are cast forth as a branch and are withered. Men gather such and cast such into the fire, and they are burned (Jn. 15:6).

COME BACK TO THE CROSS

The only solution for the church, as it has always been the solution, is to come back to the Cross. Only then can we find our moorings, our destiny, our place, who we are, and what we are to do. Without the Cross of Christ as the foundation of all that we believe, we do not know where we have been, where we are, or where we are going.

There will be some, thank God, who will come back to the Cross. It's beginning to happen already! Sadly and regrettably, most won't, but some will, and they will point the way simply because they know the way.

GRACE

"The grace of our Lord Jesus Christ be with you all. Amen" (Rev. 22:21).

The phrase, *"The grace of our Lord Jesus Christ,"* presents John using the very words of Paul in his closing salutation. Paul uses it in all of his epistles in accordance with his declaration in II Thessalonians 3:17.

As should be obvious, the Holy Spirit could have ended the canon of Scripture in any manner He desired. However, He chose to end the giving of the Word of God to this world in written form by lifting up the grace of our Lord Jesus Christ. What a blessing!

It could have ended with judgment, but instead, it ended with grace. It could have ended with hell, but instead, it ended with heaven. It could have ended with sin, but instead, it ended with salvation, for there is no other way for poor mortal man to be saved than by the redemptive grace of our Lord Jesus Christ. The law came by Moses, but grace and truth came by Jesus Christ.

The simple definition of grace is that it is "unmerited favor."

That is certainly correct; however, perhaps it would be better defined by saying "the grace of God is simply the goodness of God extended to undeserving believers." Of course, grace extends to unbelievers, as well; however, it cannot find its full force except in the heart of faith, as should be obvious.

ALL

The short phrase, *"be with you all,"* proclaims the fact that it is the same message for all and is available to all.

Let the reader understand that grace comes to us by the means of the Cross. In fact, it cannot come any other way. So, for the believer to understand the grace of God and, thereby, be a constant recipient of the grace of God, he must have an understanding of the Cross, or else, he will frustrate the grace of God, which leads to untold difficulties (Gal. 2:21).

Let us say it again: the law came by Moses, *"but grace and truth came by Jesus Christ"* (Jn. 1:17).

AMEN

Then, the final word to the great plan of God, what else could it be? It has to be the word that will give acclaim to the finished work of Christ. It is done, and, thereby, all of heaven, along with all of the redeemed, must say *"Amen."*

This world is not my home,
I'm just a-passing through.
My treasures are laid up
Somewhere beyond the blue.
The angels beckon me
From heaven's open door,
And I can't feel at home
In this world anymore.

The written Word of God
For me is final say,
And in it I have read
Of that bright coming day,
When with the holy ones
My Saviour for me comes,
And I can't feel at home
In this world anymore.

They're all expecting me,
And that's one thing I know;
My Saviour washed my sins away,
And now I onward go;
I know He'll take me through
Though I am weak and poor,
And I can't feel at home
In this world anymore.

REFERENCES

CHAPTER 2

George Williams, *William's Complete Bible Commentary*, Grand Rapids, Kregel Publications, 1994, pg. 1052.

W.A. Criswell, *The W.A. Criswell Sermon Library*, http://www. wacriswell.com/sermons/1963/the-heavenly-city-of-god/

CHAPTER 4

George Williams, *William's Complete Bible Commentary*, Grand Rapids, Kregel Publications, 1994, Pg. 1057.

W.A. Criswell, *The Right To The Tree Of Life*, Revelation 22:14, 1963, http://www.wacriswell.com/transcript/?thisid=96E-9CA9A-DA97-431C-B64FA58FBF5F2A10

George Williams, *William's Complete Bible Commentary*, Grand Rapids, Kregel Publications, 1994, Pg. 1057.

CHAPTER 5

Albert Barnes, *Notes, Explanatory and Practical, on the Book of Revelation*, Harper & Brothers, 1859, Pg. 502.

George Williams, *William's Complete Bible Commentary, Grand Rapids*, Kregel Publications, 1994, Pg. 1058.

Ibid.

Ibid.

ABOUT EVANGELIST JIMMY SWAGGART

The Rev. Jimmy Swaggart is a Pentecostal evangelist whose anointed preaching and teaching has drawn multitudes to the Cross of Christ since 1955.

As an author, he has written more than 50 books, commentaries, study guides, and The Expositor's Study Bible, which has sold more than 2.5 million copies.

As an award-winning musician and singer, Brother Swaggart has recorded more than 50 gospel albums and sold nearly 16 million recordings worldwide.

For more than six decades, Brother Swaggart has channeled his preaching and music ministry through multiple media venues including print, radio, television and the Internet.

In 2010, Jimmy Swaggart Ministries launched its own cable channel, SonLife Broadcasting Network, which airs 24 hours a day to a potential viewing audience of more than 1 billion people around the globe.

Brother Swaggart also pastors Family Worship Center in Baton Rouge, Louisiana, the church home and headquarters of Jimmy Swaggart Ministries.

Jimmy Swaggart Ministries materials can be found at **www.jsm.org**.

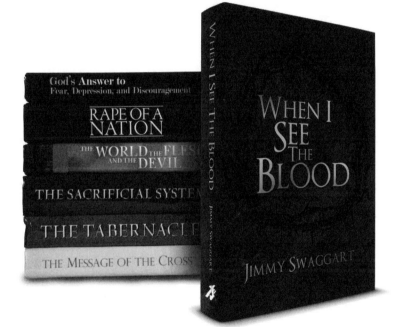